PAPER LIGHTNING

PREWRITING ACTIVITIES THAT SPARK CREATIVITY AND HELP STUDENTS WRITE EFFECTIVELY

TABLE OF CONTENTS

ORAL STORYTELLING
ORAL STORYTELLING

USING STRONG WORDS
BILLIONS AND BILLIONS TO ONE-AND-ONLY-ONE
GETTING RID OF "NOTHING" WORDS
ACTING OUT

ADDING DETAILS
SENSORY DETAILS
SENSORY WORD BANK
PACKED WITH FACTS #1 AND #2
PACKED WITH FACTS WORD BANK

UGLY WRITING
UGLY WRITING

ORGANIZING FACTS
"SORTING" EXERCISES
MORE IDEAS

PLANNING TO PERSUADE
AGREEMENT/DISAGREEMENT WALL

(continued)

TABLE OF CONTENTS, *continued*

INTRODUCTION

I do two things: I write and I teach writing.

My writing encompasses children's picture books, children's novels, children's nonfiction, blogs, and freelance articles about writing, teaching writing, and quilting. I've taught writing for seven years at a local university and provided professional development classes for over twenty years to elementary through high school teachers. I've taught writing to kids and I've taught "Novel Revision Retreat" workshops nationwide for over eight years to advanced adult writers.

With all this writing and all this teaching of writing, I have found that prewriting exercises help individuals become better writers. Prewriting is all the thinking and planning that goes on before someone actually sits down to write. It's the most neglected step of the writing process, but it has the potential to make the most difference in a student's writing.

The activities in *Paper Lightning* stimulate thought, reflection, memories, and research. They help students try out words and phrases and choose effective language. They help them organize and structure their work. They help them generate material while addressing both structure and language.

Strong prewriting activities alone can't guarantee strong results. But strong prewriting activities set the stage for strong first drafts, which have a jump start in the revision process. Good writing involves an intimate struggle with language and a passion to communicate effectively. By beginning this struggle in the prewriting stage, we focus a student's attention not just on what is said, but on how it is said.

In other words, we direct each student to pay attention to his or her own voice.

— Darcy Pattison

ACKNOWLEDGMENTS

Thanks to my editor Cheryl Thurston and her staff, who have helped me clarify my thoughts and speak more effectively to the audience of teachers.

CORRELATIONS

6 + 1 Traits ® Writing Correlation

	IDEAS AND CONTENT	ORGANIZATION	VOICE	SENTENCE FLUENCY	WORD CHOICE	CONVENTIONS	PRESENTATION
Oral Storytelling	X	X	X	X	X		
Using Strong Words	X		X		X		
Adding Details	X		X		X		
Ugly Writing	X		X		X		
Organizing Facts	X	X					
Planning to Persuade	X	X			X		
Planning Fiction	X	X	X		X		
Folk Tales	X		X				

Scaffolded Writing. With minor modifications, most of the activities in *Paper Lightning* are appropriate for use anywhere along the continuum of shared writing to independent writing. The strategies give writers a support structure that gives them confidence as they move toward independence.

NCTE (National Council of Teachers of English) Beliefs About the Teaching of Writing. The activities in *Paper Lightning* support NCTE's statement about the teaching of writing. (www.ncte.org/about/over/positions/category/write/118876.htm)

Writer's Workshop. With minor modifications, most of the activities in *Paper Lightning* are appropriate for mini-lessons with a Writer's Workshop methodology. They are especially appropriate at the beginning of a new writing task.

ORAL
STORYTELLING
■ ■ ■

One of the hardest things for students to do is to choose an appropriate topic to write about. It is also often hard for them to know what to say about a topic after they have chosen it. Because "Oral Storytelling" is done orally, without committing words to paper, students are free to explore several topics. They also generate material to write about, without even realizing it.

Having students tell stories to friends is the most natural way to try out the power of prewriting.

ORAL STORYTELLING
Rehearsing a story

Overview. With "Oral Storytelling," students team up to tell each other stories. Rehearsing a story orally helps them put things in order, select details and gauge audience reaction. They receive feedback before they begin to commit a story to writing.

Ultimately, students are going to tell five stories. The first three are different stories. Then they choose one of those three stories and tell it differently two more times. That story is the one they will ultimately write about.

Getting started. Go over the rules on the student instruction sheet for choosing a story to tell and give students a few minutes to choose their stories.

After everyone has a story, have students break into pairs for storytelling. (A group of three is okay for an odd number of participants, but be sure to adjust the times so that each person has enough time to talk.)

Telling the story. Next, students tell their stories to their partners. Each has a minute and a half to tell his or her story, with a verbal warning at the one-minute mark.

Telling a second story. Have students now choose a second story to tell. Students will probably groan, but that's okay. I always laugh and tell them that I know it's hard, but they should just try. I encourage them by pointing out that all of them have many personal experiences in their lives to tell about. They always manage.

Students tell their second stories to their partners. Again, each has a minute and a half to tell the story, with a verbal warning at the one-minute mark.

Note: You might think it's better to tell the students up front that they must come up with three ideas, but the psychology of finding and telling stories works better if you do each separately. The students need to commit to each story and tell it the best they can.

After they tell the first story, though, they are in a different position. They have now told a story to a real audience and seen how the audience reacted, what kinds of questions it had, where it might have been confused. They can change in response to what they have experienced. They can use what they have just learned about audience.

I rarely stop and ask the students to discuss what they learned by telling a story to a real audience, but that's possible. Did it help to have someone listening? Did they notice where the story kept the listener's attention? Did they notice where the listener stopped paying attention? How can they change the way they tell the story to keep the listener's interest better?

Telling a third story. Have students now choose a third story to tell. They will probably need even more encouragement, but they can do it. Again, each student has a minute and a half each to tell his or her story, with a verbal warning at the one-minute mark.

ORAL STORYTELLING, *continued*

Revising the story orally. Now the process changes. Ask students to do the following:

- **Tell the story a different way.** Ask students to choose their favorite of the three stories they have just told and tell it again—but in a different way and for a longer period of time. They might begin at a different place and/or end at a different place. They might slow down the action and tell it in much more detail. They might imagine they are telling the story to a specific audience. (The way you tell about a car wreck changes when you tell it to your mom, the cop, and your best friend.) They might tell about the weather, the colors, the smells, etc. They might add dialogue.

  Allow three minutes for storytelling this time, (1-1/2 minutes for each person) with verbal warnings at one and a half, two, and two and a half minutes.

  After the stories, have all the listeners fill in answers to the Feedback #1 questions, page 12, and share the answers with the storytellers.

- **Tell it a different way—again.** At the risk of student rebellion, ask students to tell their stories again, but this time, they must stretch them out to three minutes each.

  Allow six minutes for storytelling this time, (3 minutes for each person) with verbal warnings at one and a half, two, and two and a half minutes.

Writing. Finally, the last step is for students to tell the last story again, but this time in writing. With the practice they have had in telling the story, the will probably find it fairly easy to write.

This exercise encapsulates much of what we want students to learn about writing: to consider the audience, to expand, to revise. It also reinforces attitudes we want, such as openness to revision.

ORAL STORYTELLING

You are going to tell a story, aloud. You will eventually write this story, so keep that in mind as you think about what story to tell.

What story should you tell? In choosing a story to tell, keep the following rules in mind:

- It must be about something that really happened to you.

- It must be about something that took place in about a 30-minute time period. Otherwise, your story won't be focused enough. (Instead of telling about the three days you spent at a theme park, tell about what you did during the half hour you spent in line for the roller coaster.)

- In the story, you must be doing something active—for example, riding a horse, playing a sport, cooking, playing a game, taking a walk. If you were sitting back and watching something happen to someone else, your story is not a good one for this exercise.

    You might think a car wreck or a visit to an emergency room would make a good story. In these situations, though, *you* are usually reacting to what another person is doing. It's better to choose a story where you are doing the main action. Telling about playing a video game doesn't work well, either, because your only action is moving a controller. Instead, choose something where you are doing something more active.

- The story does not have to be a huge, overwhelming event. Simple events work well, if there is lots of action. For example, write about washing a car, climbing a tree, riding a roller coaster, fishing, playing soccer, riding a horse for the first time, etc.

Feedback #1. Listen to your partner's story. Then, complete these sentences:

1. One thing I liked about this story was _____

2. I got confused when_____

3. I'd like to know more about _____

Feedback #2. Listen to your partner's revised story. Then, complete these sentences.

1. One thing I liked about this story was _____

2. I got confused when_____

3. I'd like to know more about _____

USING
STRONG
WORDS

■ ■ ■

When students read the following sets of sentences, they can usually tell you which set is better. They may not be able to tell you *why*, though.

Set 1: The big cat is in the green tree.
        The angry cat is meowing loudly.
        The yellow cat is very hungry.

Set 2: The Siamese leapt into the oak.
        The tabby yowled.
        The Maine Coon cat gobbled the catfish.

The reason, of course, is that the second set focuses on specific nouns and active verbs. Most readers prefer the second set of sentences because it gives them a better image of what is happening.

Good writing uses strong vocabulary. This section will help students learn to use strong nouns and verbs. It will help them learn the habit of thinking about their word choices.

BILLIONS-AND-BILLIONS TO ONE-AND-ONLY-ONE
Using strong nouns and modifiers

Overview. Students often mistakenly think that they will strengthen their writing by just adding a lot of modifiers to a vague noun. "Billions-and-Billions to One-and-Only-One" helps students see the importance of choosing a strong noun and then strengthening it with specific details.

Getting Started. With your class, read aloud and discuss the student instructions for "Billions-and-Billions to One-and-Only-One." It introduces the concept of billions-and-billions nouns, which are nouns so general that they can't create a specific picture. With a billions-and-billions noun, there are billions and billions of possibilities.

By choosing a more specific noun and then specific words to describe it, writers go from billions-and-billions to one-and-only-one.

Suggestion. Once students are familiar with the process of turning billions-and-billions nouns into one-and-only-one descriptions, you can practice orally. At the end of class or at other odd times, use five minutes to have students practice going from billions-and-billions to one-and-only-one. You might even want to choose teams and keep a running tally for a week.

Discussion. When is it okay to use general nouns? Sometimes, a general noun is the right word to use. As with all writing, it depends on context and the writer's purpose. Generally, writing improves when nouns are as specific as possible.

BILLIONS-AND-BILLIONS TO ONE-AND-ONLY-ONE

If someone says the word *fish*, do you have a good picture in your head of what that fish looks like?

No. There are billions and billions of fish in the world.

Does it help to say *big* fish?

Not much. There are still billions and billions of big fish in the world.

How about if we substitute *catfish* for fish? Do you have a good picture in your head what that looks like?

Better. A catfish is more specific, but there are still millions and millions of catfish in the world.

How about if we say, "An ancient catfish who wears five hooks in his mouth as proof that he escaped fishermen five different times"? Now do you have a good picture in your head of what that fish looks like?

Yes. After you have a specific noun—*catfish*—then you can add other details to complete the picture for the reader.

Instructions. In two steps, change each billions-and-billions noun below into a specific one-and-only-one description.

Example
Billions-and-billions noun: *dog*
More specific noun: *poodle*
One-and-only-one description: *splotchy black poodle that has been rolling around in red mud*

1. Billions-and-billions noun: *shoes*
   More specific: _____
   One-and-only-one description: _____

   _____

2. Billions-and-billions noun: *bread*
   More specific: _____
   One-and-only-one description: _____

   _____

3. Billions-and-billions noun: *color*
   More specific: _____
   One-and-only-one description: _____

   _____

STUDENT INSTRUCTIONS

4. Billions-and-billions noun: *bird*
   More specific: _____
   One-and-only-one description: _____

   _____

5. Billions-and-billions noun: *truck*
   More specific: _____
   One-and-only-one description: _____

   _____

6. Billions-and-billions noun: *building*
   More specific: _____
   One-and-only-one description: _____

   _____

7. Billions-and-billions noun: *pencil*
   More specific: _____
   One-and-only-one description: _____

   _____

8. Billions-and-billions noun: *cloth*
   More specific: _____
   One-and-only-one description: _____

   _____

9. Billions-and-billions noun: *pants*
   More specific: _____
   One-and-only-one description: _____

   _____

10. Billions-and-billions noun: *machine*
    More specific: _____
    One-and-only-one description: _____

    _____

GETTING RID OF "NOTHING" WORDS
Using strong adjectives

Overview. "Nothing" words are words that add nothing new to a description. This exercise helps students recognize and learn to eliminate "nothing" adjectives. (Other exercises will help students with "nothing" verbs and adverbs. See pages 20 and 21.)

Getting started. Talk with students about choosing strong adjectives to go with strong nouns. (If they have completed "Billions-and-Billions to One-and-Only-One," they should have some understanding of strong nouns.) The weakest writing uses a general noun plus a "nothing" word. But a strong noun plus a "nothing" word still needs improvement. Help the students understand the following:

1. Adjectives should tell something specific about the noun. For example, *the freshly-cut grass* tells the reader about the height of the grass.

2. Adjectives should add new information. For example, *the green grass* adds nothing new to the reader's understanding of grass because most grass is green. However, *patchy grass* gives new information.

3. Generic adjectives like "good" or "nice" add nothing new to the description. Instead of *nice* grass, a description might read *dense, neatly-manicured emerald green grass.*

Name _____

GETTING RID OF "NOTHING" ADJECTIVES

Adjectives should tell something specific about a noun. When an adjective adds nothing new to the description, it is a "nothing" word.

Here are a few examples of "nothing" words:

good, bad, pretty, fun, exciting, awesome, cool, gorgeous, nice, easy

Instructions. Underline the "nothing" word in each sentence below. Then rewrite the sentence to replace the "nothing" word with one or two stronger adjectives:

Example

We ate lunch in a pretty cafeteria. (*Pretty* says nothing specific about the cafeteria.)
We ate lunch in a remodeled, sunny cafeteria. (*Remodeled* tells the reader that the cafeteria has probably been spiffed up. *Sunny* tells it is probably bright and cheerful.)

1. Hunter went to a cool restaurant with his friends to celebrate his birthday.

_____

_____

2. For lunch, they ate good chili.

_____

_____

3. After lunch, the waiter carried out a big cake.

_____

_____

4. Everyone thought the cake was nice.

_____

_____

5. His friends sang "Happy Birthday." Their voices were bad, and everyone laughed.

_____

_____

Now write another sentence about the party, using at least one strong adjective.

_____

_____

_____

ACTING OUT
Using strong verbs and adverbs

Overview. One element of strong writing is strong, specific verbs. Good writers use the most specific verb possible and then add modifiers only if really needed. "Acting Out" helps students learn to use strong verbs.

Getting started. Talk with students about using strong verbs. You might use the following illustration:

Does the verb in each of the following sentences communicate effectively?

1. The girl *moved* across the room.
    No. *Moved* is a rather wishy-washy verb.

2. The girl *limped* across the room. Better. *Limped* gives a more exact picture of the action. Of course, she might also *trudge, amble, march,* etc.

3. The boy *moved slowly* across the room.
    No. *Move* is still too wishy-washy, and trying to fix it by adding an adverb is the wrong solution. The best solution is to use a strong verb.

4. The boy *strolled* across the room. Yes. The strong verb—*strolled*—gives a strong picture.

5. The boy *strolled casually* across the room.
    Maybe. In this case, *casually* is probably unnecessary. Sometimes a strong verb is enough, without the adverb.

Activity. Clear a large space on one side of the classroom and ask the students to line up along that side. One at a time, a student moves across the room and demonstrates a verb that might replace *move* in this sentence: *The student moved across the room.* The other students will guess what verb is being acted out.

This is a fun, if sometimes rowdy, exercise that emphasizes the physical nature of verbs. It grounds the verb in the human body and lets students feel the importance of a verb. Once they have felt the difference between a limp and a stroll, they are more likely to make similar changes in their writing.

Suggested verbs to act out. If desired, you can write the following verbs on index cards and give them to students to act out:

dash, hop, skip, jump, crawl, skate, creep, dance, march, stomp, tiptoe, strut, parade, prance, jog, dance, stumble, limp, lope, hobble, roll, dribble, dodge, shuffle, stagger, leap, sashay, swagger, sprint, dart, gallop, trot.

Discussion. Is it ever okay to use general verbs? Yes, sometimes a general verb or a "to be" verb is the right verb to use. It depends on the context and the author's intentions. (Sometimes a character really does just *walk* and not *lumber* or *skip*.) In general, though, writing improves when the most specific verb is chosen.

Follow-up. After students are more familiar with strong verbs and adverbs, follow up with "Getting Rid of 'Nothing' Verbs" and "Getting Rid of 'Nothing' Adverbs" on pages 20 and 21.

GETTING RID OF "NOTHING" VERBS

When you want a strong verb, the "to be" or "state of being" verbs are often not the best choice. The "to be" verbs are:

is, be, am, are, was, were, been, being

These "nothing" words can often be replaced with strong, active verbs. It is not wrong to use any of these words, and sometimes they really are the best choice. However, it's always a good idea to check to see if another verb would paint a more active picture.

Instructions. Underline the "to be" verb in each sentence below. Rewrite the sentence using a strong verb. Then add other details to make the sentence more interesting.

> **Example**
> Original: *The ringmaster was loud.*
> Improved: *With a booming voice, the ringmaster announced the trapeze act.*

1. The clown's voice was funny.
   _____
   _____

2. The horses were fast.
   _____
   _____

3. Inside the circus tent, a woman was sick.
   _____
   _____

4. Elephants are always hungry.
   _____
   _____

5. The circus band was noisy.
   _____
   _____

Now write another sentence about the circus, using a strong verb.
   _____
   _____

Name _____

GETTING RID OF "NOTHING" ADVERBS

When an adverb adds nothing new to the description, it is a "nothing" word. Some common "nothing" adverbs are these:

really, very, usually, obviously, truly, fairly, certainly, simply, quite

Sometimes, you can replace these "nothing" adverbs with stronger words. However, it is often best just to eliminate them altogether.

Instructions. Underline the "nothing" verbs and adverbs in each sentence below. Change the verb to a stronger verb. Then decide if you want to eliminate the weak adverb or change it to a strong one. Rewrite each sentence in the space provided.

Example
The greyhound *ran* very quickly across the road.
The greyhound *sprinted* across the road.
> or
The greyhound *sprinted energetically* across the road.

1. At the dog show, the judges looked carefully at every dog.

   _____

   _____

2. The German shepherd walked very slowly around the ring.

   _____

   _____

3. The dalmatian jumped easily onto the chair.

   _____

   _____

4. After waking up, the golden retriever was hungry and quickly ate his food.

   _____

   _____

5. Sitting on a girl's lap, the Chihuahua slept very soundly.

   _____

   _____

Now write another sentence about the dog show, using a strong verb.

   _____

   _____

ADDING
DETAILS
■ ■ ■

One common failing of beginning writers is that they use general instead of specific details. However, this is one area where simple instruction can make a huge difference in student writing.

On the following pages are two types of prewriting activities that help students generate details in a variety of writing situations:

- The exercises about using sensory details (pages 25-28) provide easy ways for students to notice the world around them through the five senses. These exercises can be used to help students when they are writing descriptive essays, narrative essays, fiction, expository essays, and some parts of persuasive essays.

- The exercises about using specific details (pages 29-34) help students when sensory details are limited or unavailable—generally when writing is more abstract and deals with concepts or ideas. These exercises can be used to help students when they are writing expository essays and persuasive essays.

Sometimes, you can use both kinds of activities for a piece of writing because both kinds of details are appropriate.

SENSORY DETAILS
Using details from the five senses

Overview. As human beings, we understand the world around us through our senses: seeing, hearing feeling, touching, smelling. Good writing includes sensory details as a way to ground the reading experience in our bodies. "Sensory Details" gives students practice in recognizing details from the five senses.

Background. Before beginning the exercises, review with your students the types of details used for each sense.

- Seeing (visual details): colors, shapes, textures, movement, etc.

  blue, square, fluffy, zipping by

- Hearing (auditory details): pitch, loudness, timbre, tone, etc.

  bass, blasting, squeaky, angry

- Tasting (gustatory details): sour, bitter, sweet, salty, or any combination of these.

  lemon, unsweetened chocolate, bacon

- Smelling (olfactory details): spicy, sharp, smoky, sweet, etc.

  bonfire, chili, roses, spoiled milk

- Feeling (tactile details) and how it feels to move in space (kinesthetic details): temperature and texture; speed, direction, intensity, etc.

  freezing, velvety, kicking, twirling

Explain that sometimes a word or phrase can evoke more than one sense:

He sneezed, or tried to, but the gag muffled the sound.

He sneezed might be a sound detail (achoo), a feeling detail (the head moving back, then forward as the sneeze comes), or a visual detail (watching the person's head movement and the hand come up to cover the mouth and nose), or all three.

Getting started. With your students, read through the instructions on "Sensory Details." Students use either colors or symbols to mark the sensory details used in the boxed passage.

Discussion. When students finish, discuss:

- How many senses are represented? Does the passage have a variety of sensory details?

- Are the details specific? Good writing uses specific details, not generalities. (Remind students of the "Billions-and-Billions to One-and-Only-One" exercise, page 15-16.)

- Does every situation need every type of sense? When would the sense of taste be best used? The sense of smell? What sense would be the easiest to add to some situations? The hardest?

Going further. Choose excerpts from any novel or other material that the class is reading and repeat the "Sensory Details" activity by marking the sensory details with color or symbols. Discuss how the author uses sensory details in his or her writing.

SENSORY DETAILS

Details from the five senses can bring a story alive. What sensory details do you see in the passage below? Mark them as follows.

- Things you see (visual details)
  Color them red, or underline them.

- Things you smell (olfactory details)
  Color them blue, or draw a rectangle around them.

- Things you taste (gustatory details)
  Color them green, or circle them.

- Things you hear (auditory details)
  Color them yellow, or draw a squiggly line underneath them.

- Things you feel (tactile details: temperature, texture) or how it feels to move in space (kinesthetic details)
  Color them purple, or enclose them in parentheses.

In this passage, David is looking around a hotel lobby and trying to find his father:

David wandered down the musty hallway toward the hotel lobby. What secrets did this old place hide behind each door? David wanted to open every one. He stopped at the last door, a turquoise blue one. A dull brass number read "1." He listened. Silence. He put a hand on the doorknob, but couldn't make himself turn it. Quickly, he turned away, and winced as the floor squeaked. No reaction from anywhere.

Silence, again. This was the quietest place he'd ever been, except for a church. Somewhere in the hotel, food was cooking, spreading a spicy aroma that made David's stomach growl. He had no idea where to find either his father or the food. His earlier anger returned and he clenched his fists: why had Father left him alone in this strange place?

SENSORY WORD BANK
Using details from the five senses

Overview. When they are writing, it is common for students to focus on visual details: size, color, shape, etc. But writing with only visual details is often weak writing. "Sensory Word Bank" helps students look for details with multiple senses, creating a word bank to use later when writing on a designated topic. It can be used before nearly any writing assignment.

Getting started. Choose a writing assignment suitable for your students, preferably something involving a lot of action. For example, you might ask them to write a description of the last minute of a sports event.

Then lead them through the student activity, step by step.

Discussion. Discuss with students which details they found easiest to add to their word banks. In general, most people think visual details are the easiest. A few think adding what they hear (auditory details) is the easiest. Since many people are visual or auditory learners, this is not surprising.

Taste is often voted the hardest sense to use, and including gustatory details does depend on the situation/setting of the story. For example, in a description of a holiday banquet, it's easy to add a description of taste. If the topic is "riding a roller coaster," it's harder to add taste details.

Smell (olfactory detail) is another hard sense to include, depending on the situation. For example, a locker room might evoke strong smells, while an ordinary classroom would probably evoke few smells.

Most writing topics will have opportunity for details about what a person feels (tactile or kinesthetic details), but students usually need encouragement and practice in noticing these details.

Of course, not all writing includes details from all five senses. Creating sensory word banks will help students become more observant and use sensory details that are appropriate for a particular subject.

SENSORY WORD BANK

As human beings, we understand the world around us through our senses: seeing, hearing feeling, touching, smelling. You may have heard the old saying, "Show, don't tell." This exercise helps you do exactly that. Sensory details help readers feel like they are experiencing the situation and not just hearing about it.

In this prewriting activity, you will practice noticing sensory details. You will create a "word bank" by depositing words that you can withdraw later when you write.

INSTRUCTIONS

1. **Choose your topic.** (Your teacher will give you guidelines.)

2. **Re-experience the action.** If you are writing a personal narrative, close your eyes and try to imagine that you are back in the situation as it happened. If you are writing fiction, close your eyes and try to imagine the action happening moment by moment as you watch. Slow down and let the story unfold in your mind's eye.

    As the action unfolds, notice sensory details. What do you see? Hear? Taste? Feel? Smell?

3. **Deposit words in your word bank.** Write words or phrases for each sense into your word bank. (Don't worry yet about using complete sentences). Be sure to choose specific nouns, active verbs, interesting adjectives, strong adverbs. Try to write at least three things for each sense. The better the words you deposit now, the better your story will be later.

4. **Think about each stage of the action.** If you are writing about a roller coaster ride, you might begin by thinking of details about standing in line waiting to get on the roller coaster. But as you re-experience being seated on the roller coaster, the details will change drastically. They will change again as the roller coaster starts down the tracks. You might need to repeat Step #2 and Step #3 several times as the situation you are writing about changes.

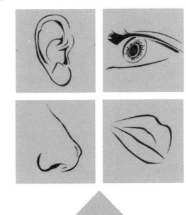

5. **Write.** When you write, keep your "Sensory Word Bank" beside you and use the words as needed. But don't be tied to it. If you think of good words or phrases as you write, use them, too.

Follow-up. Look over the words in your word bank. What kind of sensory details are easiest for you? What kind are hardest for you?

The next time you create a word bank, pay special attention to the details that are hardest for you, and try to use more of them. For example, you might think visual details are easy, but details about smell are hard. If so, then try to add more details about smell next time. Remember that good writing generally uses a variety of sensory details, not just one kind.

SENSORY WORD BANK, *continued*

Topic: _____

PACKED WITH FACTS, #1 AND #2
Using specific details

Background. Adding sensory details can greatly improve many kinds of writing. But what if it doesn't make sense to use sensory details? Expository, informational, or persuasive essays often need a different strategy for adding details. They are usually more abstract, often involving concepts or ideas. As a result, sensory details are often limited or unavailable.

For example, if an essay is a discussion of how a state legislature is organized, there will be few appropriate sensory details. However, the writer still needs to provide specific details, or the essay will flounder.

Too general:
The Arkansas state legislature has a couple of houses with a lot of elected officials.

More specific:
The Arkansas state legislature has two branches, a House of Representatives and a Senate. The House of Representatives has 100 members, while the Senate has 35 members.

The second example uses statistics, proper names, and details about the organizational structure of the legislature.

Getting started. Talk with students about how sensory details are not always appropriate for all kinds of writing, especially writing about concepts or ideas. Read and discuss the introduction to "Packed with Facts #1." Then have students follow the instructions for finding statistics, facts, and proper nouns in "The Gold State Coach."

Follow up. Follow the same procedure with "Packed with Facts #2." This exercise, "The Buffalo River," includes sensory details as well as statistics, facts, and proper and specific nouns. Would the writing be as interesting without the sensory details?

You might also have students note the strong verbs used in the piece. Have them imagine the writing without those verbs. Would it be as strong?

PACKED WITH FACTS #1

STUDENT INSTRUCTIONS

What makes some writing interesting and some writing boring? Often, it is the use of details from the five senses. Sometimes it is the use of other specific details, like these:

- statistics
- facts
- proper and specific nouns

Instructions. Read "The Gold State Coach," an informational poem about the royal coach of King George II of England, who ruled Britain during the Revolutionary War. The coach is still used today for British coronations.

Then do the following:

- Statistics—Color them blue (or draw a square around them).
- Other facts—Color them green (or circle them).
- Proper or specific nouns—Color them red (or underline them).

The Gold State Coach

Like Atlas's corded and muscled back,
King George's coach was simply colossal.
Twenty-four feet in length and thirteen high,
Eight-foot three-inches wide: it weighed four tons.

The coach's framework was made of eight palm trees
Which branched to support the roof. At each corner
A lion's head proclaimed British triumphs.
Three cherubs on top represented England,
Scotland, Ireland; the three together
Supported the Royal Crown. The coach's body
Was leather-slung between four gold sea-gods;
Massive wheels bore this Monarch of Oceans.
Painted, gilded, ornate, and triumphal–
George's royal coach was simply superb.

From the royal stables at Hampton Court,
came buff-colored Hanoverian creams:
pale manes and tails, they stood seventeen hands.
Though jostled through the noisy, crowded streets,
Eight strong, they pulled the massive coach with calm
and steady treads. With pageantry, King George
rode proud. And when the Empire's weight and wealth
passed by, even the very earth trembled.

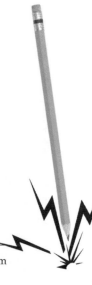

PACKED WITH FACTS #2

What makes some writing interesting and some writing boring? As discussed in "Packed with Facts #1," it is often the use of details from the five senses. Sometimes it is the use of other specific details, like these:

- statistics
- facts
- proper nouns or specific nouns

Instructions. Read the informational piece, "The Buffalo River," below. It includes statistics, facts, proper nouns and specific nouns, *and* sensory details. Then do the following:

- Highlight statistics in blue (or draw a square around them).
- Highlight facts in green (or circle them).
- Highlight proper nouns or specific nouns in red (or underline them).
- Highlight any sensory details in yellow (or draw a squiggly line under them).

The Buffalo River

One day, I put on an orange life preserver and stepped into an aluminum canoe to float the Buffalo River, a 132-mile river that winds through the Ozark Mountains of Arkansas. In 1972, Congress named it our first National River.

The river was wide and slow moving. Through clear depths, I spied small-mouth bass feeding. Several red-eared sliders, which were sunning on a fallen log, slipped into the water. Coming around a limestone bluff, I surprised great blue herons, which took off in a whir of wings. The sun didn't bother me most of the time because the canoe glided in and out of the shade of oak and hickory branches. Squirrels chattered at me; chickadees and titmouse birds scolded me. Black snakes, which were basking on overhanging limbs, slid off into the water when I came close.

PACKED WITH FACTS WORD BANK
Using specific details

Overview. With this activity, students create a word bank by filling in a chart that asks for facts, statistics, proper nouns and specific nouns. It is an excellent prewriting activity to use when students are writing reports or essays that involve information, concepts, and/or ideas.

Getting started. Assign a writing task of your choice to students, one that does not lend itself to sensory details and which will likely need some research on the part of students. A report on a subject you are studying is appropriate, for example.

Then explain that with "Packed with Facts Word Bank," they will create a word bank they will use later to help them write their papers.

Go over the instructions with students and be available for questions and help as they complete their charts.

PACKED WITH FACTS WORD BANK

STUDENT INSTRUCTIONS

Sometimes it is difficult to use sensory details, especially when your writing topic is abstract, like an idea or concept. Instead, you may want to use different specific details, such as statistics, facts, and proper or specific nouns.

Creating a "Packed with Facts Word Bank" can help. As you research your topic and find specific details, you will deposit words and phrases in your bank. You can withdraw the words and phrases later when you write.

INSTRUCTIONS

1. **Choose your topic.** (Your teacher will give you guidelines.)

2. **Write down what you already know.** List what you already know about your topic. Put the information in the appropriate column: statistics, facts, or proper or specific nouns. Write words or phrases, not complete sentences.

3. **Fill in the blanks.** Do you have enough specific details in each column to write something interesting? You may need to do research and collect more specific details from your sources. As you research, write down statistics, facts, and proper or specific nouns in the appropriate columns. Also look for interesting words that are used to discuss your topic.

   Try to find at least three things for each type of detail on the chart. The better the words and facts you deposit now, the better your writing will be later.

4 **Write.** When you write, keep the "Packed with Facts Word Bank" beside you and use the words as you need them. Don't be tied to it, though. If you realize you forgot to write down someone's complete name, for example, be sure to go and look it up in your sources.

PACKED WITH FACTS WORD BANK, *continued*

Topic: _____

Statistics	Facts	Proper or Specific Nouns (and how they relate to the topic)

UGLY
WRITING
■ ■ ■

Our goal in teaching writing is "lovely" student writing—writing that is interesting, well-articulated, coherent, and free of grammar or spelling mistakes. We reach for this goal by giving students models of good writing. However, sometimes students don't see the gap between the models and what they write themselves. Until they see the weakness in their own writing, they are unlikely to change and improve.

"Ugly Writing" helps them see their own weaknesses as they first try to produce bad writing. The experience of removing the "good stuff" from a piece of writing helps them see, in a backwards way, what they need to do to improve.

UGLY WRITING
A review of using strong words and details

Overview. With this fun-to-do activity, students are asked to deliberately "write ugly." They take a well-written passage and rewrite it, removing the strong words and details in a "backwards" demonstration of what makes effective writing.

The activity reviews the need for strong words and effective details and looks at how these work together to produce strong writing.

Modeling the exercise. First do a demonstration of "Ugly Writing" by completing a sample activity with students.

Read aloud to your class the example of strong writing in Box A, below. (You may want to reproduce it on an overhead transparency, for ease of discussion.) Ask students, as they listen, to notice the strong words (verbs, nouns, adjectives, adverbs) and strong details (sensory details, statistics, facts, and proper or specific nouns).

Discussion. Discuss with students the writing in the passage. Notice that nouns are specific. There are many strong verbs and few "to be" verbs. There are many sensory details.

Continuing the model. Finally, show students how the passage would read *without* strong words and details. Read aloud the "Ugly" example in Box B, page 37. It eliminates strong nouns and verbs and specific adjectives and adverbs. It inserts "to be" verbs. It removes sensory details, statistics, facts, and proper and specific nouns.

Discussion. Do the original version and the ugly version have the same information? What is the difference?

Students should easily be able to see that the example in Box A includes strong words and details.

A | **Strong.** The following passage describes a boy trying to shoot an owl with a tranquilizer dart, so he can collect feathers to sell.

Micah stretched upward – bit by bit – until he could see the barred-owl roosting in the pine tree only twenty feet away. A damp breeze whispered through the live oak in which he hid, making a twig tickle his cheek. He ignored it. For the last thirty minutes he had been stalking the owl through the grove, moving into the perfect position to take a shot, and he wasn't about to make a sudden move now. While he waited, dark branches took on a chocolate color in the growing dawn. The next time the wind lifted the leaves around him, he took a deep breath and brought the bamboo tube to his lips. Then he blew hard. Before the poison-tipped dart fell just short of the owl, Micah knew his aim was off and had another dart out of his belt pack and loaded into the tube.

UGLY WRITING, *continued*

B | **Ugly.**

The boy saw a big bird in a tree. The wind was really quiet. He didn't notice. He had been watching the bird fly through the trees and was really trying to be very still, so he could shoot it. The sun was coming up slowly. The boy blew a dart at the bird, but it missed. Very, very quickly, he pulled out another dart and was ready to blow the dart at the bird again.

Completing "Ugly Writing." Pass out "Ugly Writing #1," page 38, and explain that students will follow the same steps as in the sample exercise just completed. They will rewrite the sample passage, changing it to an "ugly" version, following the steps outlined.

Sample answers. The rewritten passages will vary, but they should resemble the following:

Ugly Writing #1.

In the summer, a dog was living with us. We have a big house and yard. Dogs like to run there. But Mom likes plants. The dog could run under the trees, but could tear up plants, too.

I took the dog to the backyard. I ran and she followed. I ran even faster and she followed. I ran very, very, very fast and she followed. It was easy for the dog to run. She stopped to smell a plant.

Follow up. Pass out "Ugly Writing #2, page 39, and follow the same procedure. The rewritten passage should resemble the following:

Ugly Writing #2.

I was looking at flowers and forgot to watch where I was stepping. I stepped in snow and got my socks wet. I got my fingers wet too, when I tried to flick off the snow.

Then I heard thunder and saw lightning. I was lost at 12,000 feet.

It started to hail. I got even wetter, but I didn't care because I enjoyed watching the storm.

UGLY WRITING #1

1. Take a close look at the passage in the box below. Circle all the sensory details. Underline the strong verbs and strong nouns. Put a square around strong adjectives and adverbs.

Road Whiz strutted regally into the backyard, with her head held high, like she was balancing a crown. Her long pointed muzzle lifted to sniff.

Across the fifteen feet of lawn, the yellow rose bushes basked in the brilliant July sun. I sniffed, too. It had been a while since I noticed that sweet rose smell. Whiz tugged at her red leash and her claws clicked on the brick patio.

Mom would kill me if I let Whiz tear up her flowers. Worried, I stroked Whiz's soft ears. Greyhounds needed to run, though, so what could I do? I would have to run with her.

Click. I unsnapped the leash from her collar.

For speed, a greyhound's long, muscular legs depend on the lungs housed in the wide chest. This time, though, Whiz's chest didn't expand at all before she bounded away, floating over the springy grass. But when I followed, the grass tugged at me. I stumbled and wind-milled my arms to keep from falling. The gap between Whiz and myself lengthened to two feet, five feet, twelve feet. Whiz hit the path at a lope, kicking up puffs of soft dirt.

My heart pounded in my ears. So far, she was on the path, leaving the roses alone. "Whiz! Come here, girl!"

Whiz circled a tree, then stretched out her legs, reaching for the ground so she could push off and tuck back up like a coiled spring, ready to reach and push off again. Her grace was punctuated by gentle thumps. Then, she veered off and slowed.

Whiz's black nose touched a drooping rose. Petals from Mom's award-winning yellow rose bush drifted to the ground. And before I could lunge for her collar, Whiz hiked a leg and marked the rose bush as her territory.

---

2. Now take that perfectly good passage and do this: Write ugly. In other words, remove everything that makes the passage effective. Try not to use any of the effective words you marked, above. Change strong verbs to weak verbs or "to be" verbs. Change strong nouns to general nouns. Omit strong adjectives or adverbs. Insert "nothing words" or vague adverbs like "really" or "very." If you must use an adjective or an adverb, use a general one. Omit all sensory details.

    Your rewritten passage should have the same general meaning as the one above, but it will probably sound very, very ugly. Sometimes doing the *opposite* of what you should can help you understand what you *should* do!

UGLY WRITING #2

STUDENT INSTRUCTIONS

1. Take a close look at the passage in the box below. Circle all the sensory details. Underline the strong verbs and strong nouns. Put a square around strong adjectives and adverbs.

> *Tiny alpine flowers covered the meadow in drifts of yellow. I was so enchanted, I forgot to watch where I was stepping. Even though it was the middle of June, piles of dirty snow still lay in the deep shadows. Of course, I stepped into snow that was three inches deeper than my hiking boots. I peeled off my red mittens, then bent and flicked the icy snow out of the boot but it was too late. The top of my sock was suddenly cold and wet, like my fingers. I kicked at the snow drift in irritation.*
>
> *A sudden thunder crack startled me, and I jerked back under the pines. My boots crushed the low boughs, releasing the tangy pine smell. Lightning strobed through the clouds. I groaned. If only I'd brought the map out of the van's glove box. If only I had my compass. Instead, I was lost at 12,000 feet elevation and had no idea what direction I was traveling or what direction would take me back down to the van. Lost. Could it get any worse?*
>
> *Yes.*
>
> *A white marble rolled toward the toe of my hiking boot. No, not a marble.*
>
> *A clattering made me look up. Something smacked my forehead, stinging hard and bringing tears to my eyes. Hail. I threw my hands up to cover my face, crouched and backed into a thick pine. Snow spilled from the boughs onto my hair and face, spreading fingers of cold until I was shivering in spite of my red wool sweater. My boots filled with more damp snow and water seeped down my ankle until my socks were totally soaked. But I didn't care. I put my back against the rough bark, held aside the prickly pine needles and watched the storm in wonder. My previous irritation was swept aside, replaced by a crazy exhilaration. The patter of hailstones grew to a dull roar as the sky hurled hard icy balls until four inches of hailstones suffocated the alpine flowers.*

2. Now take that perfectly good passage and do this: Write ugly. In other words, remove everything that makes the passage effective. Try not to use any of the words you marked earlier. Change strong verbs to weak verbs or "to be" verbs. Change strong nouns to general nouns. Omit strong adjectives or adverbs. Insert "nothing words" or vague adverbs like "really" or "very." If you must use an adjective or an adverb, use a general one. Omit all sensory details.

    Your rewritten passage should have the same general meaning as the one above, but it will probably sound very, very ugly. Sometimes doing the *opposite* of what you should can help you understand what you *should* do!

ORGANIZING
FACTS

■ ■ ■

In today's world of computers, finding facts is relatively easy. Handling the facts is harder. How do students synthesize the facts into one piece of writing?

This section helps students learn to organize facts in different ways for different needs and audiences.

"SORTING" EXERCISES
Categorizing information

Overview. The "Sorting" exercises ("Sorting Elephants," "Sorting Skunks," "Sorting Hummingbirds," "Sorting Chewing Gum," pages 45-52) help students learn to categorize and sort information. After they receive a set of facts on a subject, they sort the facts into logical categories. Then they order the categories, putting them in a sequence that will communicate well. Finally, they order the information within each category.

The problem with organizing. For students, organizing information can be a huge undertaking. Given only six facts about a topic, they have 720 statistically random sequences of presenting those facts!

Of course, writing isn't random, but a way to make sense of random thoughts. That's why writers need organization—to put facts into a sequence that makes sense and that communicates a coherent message. Out of the 720 random sequences, only a handful will make sense. That leaves a lot of ways for students to go wrong.

Organizing is really a three-step process:

1. **Categorizing.** First, writers learn to sort facts. They decide on similarities and differences among the facts and put them into categories. Organizing becomes easier because there are now only a few categories to organize.

2. **Arranging the categories.** Next, writers learn to order the categories. They decide on criteria for putting the categories in an order that will communicate well. They might sort the categories in chronological order, for example, or to build to a climax. They might sort by facts (least important to most important, for example, or least interesting to most interesting), or according to any other criteria that make sense for the subject at hand.

3. **Ordering the facts within a category.** Finally, they follow the same steps to order the information within each category. Again, the arrangement might be chronological, topical, most interesting, order of importance, building to a climax, etc.

The "Sorting" exercises on the next few pages help students practice organizing facts. Why does a fact fit into one category but not another? In what order should the categories be presented? Within each category, what order makes sense?

For these exercises, the discussion is important because it exposes the various ways that a writer might organize material. Often, there isn't just one right way to organize a group of facts. Rather, the organization may depend on the writer's intent. What does he or she want to communicate?

There are stronger and weaker ways of organizing. Strong organization shows the relationships among the facts and communicates those relationships with clarity.

Preparation. For each "Sorting" exercise, students will need a set of "cards" that contain facts. If students are working individually, each student will need a set of cards. If they are working in groups, each group will need just one set of cards.

(continued)

"SORTING" EXERCISES, *continued*

To prepare the cards, photocopy the fact sheets and cut apart the facts, being sure to keep each cut-apart set separate from others. (Envelopes help!) You can then use the facts as they are, or you can make them sturdier by gluing, taping, or stapling them onto note cards. (You can also have students themselves cut apart the facts.)

The "Sorting" exercises that follow have four levels:

- Easiest ("Sorting Elephants" and "Sorting Skunks"). Students categorize six facts.
- More challenging ("Sorting Hummingbirds"). Students categorize 12 facts.
- Most challenging ("Sorting Chewing Gum"). Students categorize 16 facts.

All the exercises can be adapted for either individuals or groups, but it is helpful to start in groups first. The discussion can be lively, and students can see, from the various opinions in the group, that there are various ways to organize facts. Your goal, though, is for each writer to eventually become confident working alone. ("Sorting Elephants" and "Sorting Skunks" are set up as group exercises, and "Sorting Hummingbirds" and "Sorting Chewing Gum" are set up as individual exercises.)

Getting started. Give students their set of facts. Then lead them through the steps on the student instructions.

"Using 'Sorting Elephants'" (See next column) describes one way to handle the exercise. Other "Sorting" exercises can follow a similar pattern, adapting for group or individual work.

Using "Sorting Elephants." After students read the facts about elephants, ask them to choose categories for the facts. They are likely to come up with these categories, or something similar:

Size
Elephants grow to about 13 feet tall.
Elephants can weigh as much as a school bus.

Food
Elephants eat grass, small branches and tree bark.
Elephants will knock down a tree to eat its leaves.

Travel
When elephants travel, they walk single file.

That leaves one fact: *Elephants can travel ten miles to find food.* Ask students if they would put that fact into the "food" or the "travel" category. Why?

Either category could be correct. Putting the fact in the food category emphasizes that elephants will travel to find food. Putting it into the travel category emphasizes that one reason elephants travel is to find food.

Point out that there isn't necessarily only one right answer when sorting facts into categories. But students should be able to explain *why* they put a fact into a category.

The next step is putting the categories in order. Again, there isn't necessarily only one right answer. It is important that students discuss *why* they would put categories into a specific order.

(continued)

"SORTING" EXERCISES, *continued*

For example, here are some possible reasons:

- "Size" should come first because readers need to know about the elephant's size in order to understand its food habits.

- "Travel" should come first. The most interesting fact is that elephants like to travel single file. Since it is important to catch the reader's attention right away with something interesting, "travel" should be the first category.

The third step is ordering the facts within a category. Again, there isn't necessarily one right answer, and students should discuss *why* they would put the information in a certain order. For example, they might order the facts one way if they are writing for a very young audience. They might choose another order for a science report.

A final step (optional on group exercises) is to use the sorted categories and facts as an outline for writing. If you wish, students can, individually, write a very simple report, using the facts provided. Then have them compare their reports. How are they the same, or different, depending on how students sorted the categories?

SORTING ELEPHANTS

Elephants can weigh as much as a school bus.

When elephants travel, they walk single file.

Elephants will knock down a tree to eat its leaves.

Elephants eat grass, small branches and tree bark.

Elephants grow to about 13 feet tall.

Elephants can travel ten miles to find food.

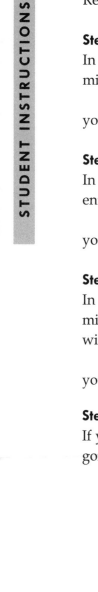

STUDENT INSTRUCTIONS

SORTING ELEPHANTS

Read over the facts you have received on elephants. Then complete the steps that follow.

Step One: Sort the facts into categories.

In your group, sort the facts into categories. To do this, first discuss the different ways you might sort the facts. Each group member may have different ideas.

Come to a group decision on the best categories. Be ready to share with the class *why* your group thinks these are the best categories.

Step Two: Order the categories.

In your group, put the categories in an order that makes sense. To do this, discuss the different ways you might order the categories. Each group member may have different ideas.

Come to a group decision on which order is best. Be ready to share with the class *why* your group thinks this is the best order.

Step Three: Order the facts within each category.

In your group, put the facts in order within each category. Discuss the different ways you might order these facts. Each group member may have different ideas on the best order within each category.

Come to a group decision on which order is best. Be ready to share with the class *why* your group thinks this is the best order.

Step Four: Use the sorting as an outline to write.

If you were actually writing a report, you could then use the sorted facts and their categories as an outline.

SORTING SKUNKS

Skunks are more active at night.

Skunks will tear into garbage bags and eat what they find.

Skunks are about 2 feet long.

Skunks locate food more by smell than by sight.

Skunks weigh about 10 pounds.

Skunks eat insects, fruits, and berries.

SORTING SKUNKS

Read over the facts you have received on skunks. Then complete the steps that follow.

Step One: Sort the facts into categories.

In your group, sort the facts into categories. To do this, first discuss the different ways you might sort the facts. Each group member may have different ideas.

Come to a group decision on the best categories. Be ready to share with the class *why* your group thinks these are the best categories.

Step Two: Order the categories.

In your group, put the categories in an order that makes sense. To do this, discuss the different ways you might order the categories. Each group member may have different ideas.

Come to a group decision on which order is best. Be ready to share with the class *why* your group thinks this is the best order.

Step Three: Order the facts within each category.

In your group, put the facts in order within each category. Discuss the different ways you might order these facts. Each group member may have different ideas on the best order within each category.

Come to a group decision on which order is best. Be ready to share with the class *why* your group thinks this is the best order.

Step Four: Use the sorting as an outline to write.

If you were actually writing a report, you could then use the sorted facts and their categories as an outline.

SORTING HUMMINGBIRDS

Hummingbirds have been caught and eaten by dragonflies.	Hummingbirds are four inches long.	Hummingbirds can get caught in spider webs.
Hummingbirds are so small that other animals eat them.	Hummingbirds have been caught and eaten by praying mantises.	Hummingbirds need to eat twice their body weight in food every day.
Hummingbirds have a wingspan of about six inches.	When hummingbirds migrate, they fly more than 1,850 miles.	Hummingbirds have been caught and eaten by frogs.
When they migrate, hummingbirds cross 600 miles of the Gulf of Mexico.	Hummingbirds weigh 1/100 of an ounce.	Hummingbirds fly south to Central America for the winter.

STUDENT INSTRUCTIONS

SORTING HUMMINGBIRDS

Read over the facts you have received on hummingbirds. (These facts apply to ruby-throated hummingbirds.) Then complete the steps that follow.

Step One: Sort the facts into categories.
Sort the facts into categories. Decide why these are the best categories. Be ready to share with the class *why* these are the best categories.

Step Two: Order the categories.
Put the categories in order. Decide why this is the best order. Be ready to share with the class *why* this is the best effective order.

Step Three: Order the facts within each category.
Put the facts in order within each category. Decide why this is the best order. Be ready to share with the class *why* this is the best order.

Step Four: Use the sorting as an outline to write.
Write a short report on ruby-throated hummingbirds. Use the sorted facts and their categories as an outline to write the report.

.

SORTING CHEWING GUM

To the gum base, manufacturers add texture.	Sometimes gum gets a crunchy outer layer.	To the gum base, manufacturers add sweeteners.	Chewing gum is easy to carry around.
Peppermint flavoring comes from a plant.	To the gum base, manufacturers add colors.	Flavors may have 10-100 chemicals.	Chewing gum can help ease tension.
All chewing gum has a gum base.	Chewing sugarless gum helps your teeth stay healthy.	Sweeteners make the gum bulky and big.	Spearmint flavoring comes from a plant.
Chewing gum can keep your breath fresh.	The gum base is the part that is not dissolved during chewing.	Sweeteners are the main ingredient in chewing gum.	To the gum base, manufacturers add flavors.

SORTING CHEWING GUM

Read over the facts you have received on chewing gum. Then complete the steps that follow.

Step One: Sort the facts into categories.

Sort the facts into categories. Decide why these are the best categories. Be ready to share with the class *why* these are the best categories.

Step Two: Order the categories.

Put the categories in order. Decide why this is the best order. Be ready to share with the class *why* this is the best effective order.

Step Three: Order the facts within each category.

Put the facts in order within each category. Decide why this is the best order. Be ready to share with the class *why* this is the best order.

Step Four: Use the sorting as an outline to write.

Write a short report on chewing gum. Use the sorted facts and their categories as an outline to write the report.

MORE IDEAS
Sorting and organizing facts

Once students are confident with the three steps of sorting and organizing information, they can use these skills in other ways. Here are some ideas for helping students extend their organization skills:

1. Give students a series of facts on a topic, each of which could be put into multiple categories. Have students decide on the best categories for the topic. Then change essay topics and ask them to choose again.

2. To a series of facts, add extra facts that don't belong. Have students sort the facts and decide which should be omitted.

3. Give students a category with too many facts. Have them select which facts are the best facts to include in writing about this category.

4. Have students order a list of facts in a specific way—chronological order, for example, or in order of strength of support for an argument.

Organizing facts is not enough, of course. It is important that students learn to write in their own words. Have students try the following after they have worked with a list of facts:

• Ask students to put away their notes and write the facts from memory. Often students resist this because they worry about spelling, so encourage them to wait until a full draft is finished before correcting spelling.

• Do a variation of "Oral Storytelling" (page 12). Have students tell the facts from memory in different ways. Oral practice in paraphrasing will help them do a better job when writing.

• To encourage variety in sentence structure, ask students to combine several facts into one sentence.

PLANNING
TO
PERSUADE

■ ■ ■

One important task of communication is to clearly lay out an opinion, with the purpose of persuading others to accept the opinion and possibly act upon it.

The following exercises help students clarify their thoughts, state an opinion clearly, and give reasons for that opinion—all as the first steps toward writing a persuasive paper.

AGREEMENT/DISAGREEMENT WALL
Where do you stand?

Overview. "Agreement/Disagreement Wall" helps students learn to state an opinion clearly. Students first write opinions on slips of paper and turn them in. The teacher then reads aloud each opinion, and students place themselves around the room according to how strongly they agree or disagree with the statement. When an opinion is not clearly stated, students will have difficulty agreeing or disagreeing.

Getting started. When people write to persuade, their overall goal is to get readers to agree with their opinion. To do that most effectively, they must (1) make sure readers understand their opinion and (2) use information that readers will find credible and believable. If they do those tasks well, the result is more likely to be persuasive.

The first step in helping readers understand an opinion is to state it clearly—a task that is often harder than it might seem.

Have students brainstorm a list of subjects people have opinions about. You might even want to do this as a group.

Then ask students to write at least one statement of opinion that someone (not necessarily them!) might use as a topic for a paper. Emphasize that the statement must be worded in such a way that a reader could agree or disagree. After an appropriate time, ask students to hand in their statements.

The Wall. Next, students evaluate the statements. Is this topic specific enough? Is it worded well?

Designate one wall of your room as the Agreement Wall and the opposite wall as the Disagreement Wall. The middle of the room is the Undecided, Neutral, or Uncommitted Area.

Take the statements students have turned in and read each statement, without using names. Ask students to move to the Agreement Wall, the Disagreement Wall, or the Undecided, Neutral Area, or Uncommitted Area, according to how they feel about the topic.

It easily becomes apparent when statements are poorly worded, with no possibility of agreeing or disagreeing. For example, you might read aloud this statement: "I want to write about state tests in schools."

Readers can't agree or disagree with that statement because it isn't specific and doesn't state an opinion. A stronger statement might be, "Students should not be required to take state tests." Readers can agree or disagree with that statement because it states an opinion.

It works well to do this activity *before* students actually decide on a topic because the activity itself will generate ideas. Hearing opinions on a variety of topics can help students come up with other topic ideas that may interest them.

WHAT IS MY OPINION?
Taking sides

Overview. This activity helps students clarify and think through their opinion on a topic before they write about it. They look at both sides of an issue and solicit the input and opinions of others.

Getting started. Ask students to select a topic for a persuasive paper and write it clearly as a statement someone could agree or disagree with. (Remind them of the Agreement/Disagreement Wall.)

Pass out "What Is My Opinion?", page 58, and have students complete the first item, which asks them to write the opinion statement they plan to use. Take some time to have students share their opinion statements with others, to see if they are stated clearly and specifically.

Coming up with reasons. There are two sides to every issue. Sometimes it helps students clarify their thinking when they contrast their opinion with the opposite point of view. Ask students to write reasons why someone might agree or disagree with the statement they have written. Allow time for this, but don't require them to finish at this point. The discussion to follow will help them complete the task.

Some will have a hard time writing the reasons for an opinion that is not their own. Stress that it is important to anticipate and deal with what the other side is likely to say on a topic. That way they can make sure to deal with those arguments.

Have students work in groups of two to four students. One person in each group reads aloud his or her opinion, and the other students help come up with reasons both for and against that opinion. Remind students that the reasons they give don't have to be their own personal reasons. At this point they are simply helping each other come up with all possible reasons for holding a certain opinion.

Time the discussions for each side of the argument, allowing a length of time that fits the needs of your group. Be sure to announce "switch" times so that the group addresses both sides of each student's topic.

Finally, have students, on their own, write down the best reasons they can think of that support their opinion, making a simple outline for the persuasive paper they will eventually write.

If you like, complete a sample activity with the class as a whole before having students attempt the exercise on their own. Write the topic on the board or overhead. Then lead a general discussion of typical reasons why a person would agree or disagree. This is a good time to let students be enthusiastic about their opinions and to let each student speak.

WHAT IS MY OPINION?

When you write to persuade, you have two main tasks: (1) to make sure readers understand your opinion, and (2) to try to get them to agree with that opinion. (And sometimes, we want them to go even farther and act on that opinion.)

You are preparing to write a persuasive paper. The following steps will help you clarify your opinion before you begin to write.

1. What is the topic of your paper? Write it as a statement that you can agree or disagree with:

   _____

   _____

2. Check with others. Is your statement clear? From reading your statement, do others know exactly what you are going to write about? Do they know exactly what your opinion is on this topic? If not, try to improve it. Write your improved version here:

   _____

   _____

3. Now look at both sides of the issue you have chosen. First list reasons why someone might agree with your opinion.

   _____

   _____

   _____

   _____

   _____

   _____

   _____

   _____

4. Now list reasons why someone might disagree. (Remember, you aren't writing what *you* think. You are writing why you think others might disagree.)

   _____

   _____

   _____

WHAT IS MY OPINION? *continued*

_____

_____

_____

_____

_____

_____

5. Now meet with others to see if they can help you think of other reasons to add to both lists.

6. Look over all the reasons for and against your opinion. Then choose what you think are the three strongest reasons that support your opinion. Write a simple outline for your paper, following this form:

My opinion:

_____

_____

_____

Reason #1 why it is true:

_____

_____

_____

Reason #2 why it is true:

_____

_____

_____

Reason #3 why it is true:

_____

_____

_____

MAKING REASONS BELIEVABLE
Getting others to agree

Overview. Students have previously come up with a topic for a persuasive paper. They have also come up with reasons for their point of view. In this activity, they work on supporting those reasons.

Getting started. Expanding or elaborating on ideas is one of the most difficult tasks for students. Students often start a persuasive discussion with a personal appeal, but they don't go on to back it up. "Making Reasons Believable" helps them come up with ways to back up their main reasons or arguments.

Depending on the skill level of the students and the kinds of topics chosen, you may want to encourage them to support their arguments with facts from their general knowledge, from personal experiences, from research—or from all three.

For example, if Bob wants to persuade his parents to allow him to get a dog, he will probably use knowledge of how his family has operated in the past, his own preferences about breeds of dogs, personal experiences with other dogs, etc. If, however, he wants to persuade the school that it can save money by implementing more recycling programs, he will probably need to supplement personal experience with some research.

Discussion. Pass out "Making Reasons Believable" and go over the ways listed to support an argument.

Then have students look at the reasons for and against their topic, which they completed in "What Is My Opinion?" Have some students share a reason, and then have the class brainstorm what ways they could support that reason. Would quoting an expert be a good idea? Whom could they quote?

How could they personalize the argument? Is there a story they could tell from their life? From someone else's life?

Should they do some research to find some statistics or facts to back up the argument?

Are there other ways students could support their points? For example, some might have moral or ethical arguments, or they might use simple logic to bring home a point.

Finally, have students come up with a basic outline for their paper, following this simple format:

Reason #1:
    Support:

Reason #2:
    Support:

Reason #3:
    Support:

For younger students, coming up with reasons and *any* kind of simple support may be enough. For older students, you may want to ask for two or three items of support for each reason.

Write. Finally, ask students to write a persuasive paper, using their outlines.

MAKING REASONS BELIEVABLE

STUDENT INSTRUCTIONS

When you are writing to persuade, it is important to tell why your reasons are good ones. You need to make it clear why others should accept your opinion. To do that, you need to provide support for your reasons. Readers often find the following methods of support persuasive:

A. Quote experts.

But who are experts? It depends on the subject you are addressing. If it is a topic having to do with school, teachers or principals might be the experts. In other cases, a scientist doing research on a subject might be an expert. In other cases, it might be someone who has personal experience with a subject, maybe even you!

If you wanted to persuade someone to stop smoking, for example, which of the following are you more likely to believe?

- Pam Laffin, a smoker who is dying because of emphysema, a lung disease.
- The president of a company that manufactures cigarettes.
- A clown for the local circus.
- A doctor who works for the United States Center for Disease Control.

B. Use specific facts and details:

In 1986, the *Journal of Personality and Social Psychology* reported on experiments about what makes people believe a lawyer's arguments in court. Jonathan Shedler and Melvin Manis from the University of Michigan invented a court case that asked people to decide whether or not Mrs. Johnson was abusive to her seven-year-old son. They wrote four versions of the court trial and asked people to read one and decide what they believed about Mrs. Johnson.

1. Version #1 argued that Mrs. Johnson was a good mother. For example, it said that she made sure her son brushed his teeth every night.
2. Version #2 also argued that Mrs. Johnson was a good mother, but this time, the details were more specific. She made sure he brushed his teeth every night with his Star Wars toothbrush that looked like Darth Vader.
3. Version #3 argued that Mrs. Johnson was a bad mother and gave only general details.
4. Version #4 argued that Mrs. Johnson was a bad mother and gave specific details.

The researchers found that the versions with the most specific details (Versions #2 and #4) were the most persuasive. Specific details such as dates, names, statistics, facts, etc., make an argument more believable.

(continued)

STUDENT INSTRUCTIONS

MAKING REASONS BELIEVABLE, *continued*

C. Personalize the argument.

A personal story, or a detailed story of someone else's experience, helps readers understand what is at stake. As Mother Teresa is quoted as saying, "If I look at the masses, I won't act. If I look at one, I will act."

Which of these would make you care more?

- One paragraph with statistics about the dangers of smoking.
- A twenty-minute film about Pam Laffin's life. She died in 2000 at the age of 31 from emphysema, a lung disease. Her two daughters were only 10 and 14 years old when their mother died.

The detailed story of how Pam Laffin started smoking, how she got sick, and how much she loved her daughters would be more personal and memorable than a simple listing of the number of people who die each year from lung cancer.

Which methods of support might work well for your topic? What experts could you consult? What specific details could you include? How could you personalize the argument?

Look over the basic outline you completed in "What Is Your Opinion?" Now add to this outline with ways you might support your reasons.

My opinion: _____

Reason #1: _____

_____

   Support: _____

_____

Reason #2: _____

_____

   Support: _____

_____

Reason #3: _____

_____

   Support: _____

_____

Use this outline now to write the first draft of your persuasive paper.

PLANNING
FICTION

■ ■ ■

The prewriting activities in "Planning Fiction" help writers with the creation of characters, plot, and setting when writing almost any type of fiction, including contemporary, science fiction and adventure stories.

LOOKING AT CHARACTERS
Roles and characteristics

Overview. This activity helps students learn a simple but effective way to create characters for a story:

Give the character a job or role and then add one weird or specific detail about the character.

Weird or specific details include characteristics that make a character distinctive— attitudes, likes, dislikes, fears, skills, habits, clothing, hobbies, anything that makes the character stand out and seem real.

Getting started: With your class, read a short children's book with some interesting characters. For each character, discuss his or her job or role in the story. What is one weird or specific detail about each?

For example, the chart below describes some of the characters in *The Journey of Oliver K. Woodman.* (See "Bibliography," page 107.)

Name	Job or Role	Second Job or Role	Weird or Specific Detail
Uncle Ray	carpenter	uncle	He makes wooden men.
Taneka	niece/daughter	letter writer	She likes knock-knock jokes.
Jackson McTavish	farmer		He loves Brahman bulls and his beloved Amelia.
Bobbi Jo	truck driver		She is funny (talking about Oliver not needing bathroom stops).
Melissa Tso	beauty queen	granddaughter	She gets tired of smiling.
Bernard Grape	lawyer	father	He is afraid of bears.

Paper Lightning • Copyright © 2008 by Darcy Pattison • Cottonwood Press, Inc. • 800-864-4297 • www.cottonwoodpress.com

SHUFFLE A CHARACTER
Creating interesting characters

Overview. "Shuffle a Character" helps students create an interesting character. Students are dealt two cards from a job/role card deck. Then they create a character based on one of the cards, adding details from a list of "Weird or Specific Details."

Getting started. Using the list on pages 66-68, create a deck of 50-100 job/role cards for characters. (You might photocopy onto card stock and simply cut into cards.) Then deal two cards to each student.

Also, pass out the "Shuffle a Character" student activity sheet, page 69, which includes the list of "Weird or Specific Details." Go over the instructions with the students and read aloud the list of characteristics. Students first choose a job or role from the two cards they have received, writing the choice in the correct blank. Then they decide on a weird or specific detail to add to their character. Using these decisions as a foundation, they answer the other questions about their character on the "Shuffle a Character" activity sheet.

beekeeper	fast food worker	glassblower	cartoonist
pig farmer	factory owner	goldsmith	composer
blacksmith	mailroom clerk	janitor	ice sculptor
cat breeder	secretary	mapmaker	sign painter
elephant trainer	baker	plumber	bank robber
hunter	bricklayer	roofer	forger
barber	butcher	saddle maker	pickpocket
cosmetician	chimney sweep	tattoo artist	smuggler
model	coffin maker	truck driver	English teacher
accountant	doll maker	weaver	Spanish teacher
bank teller	electrician	architect	librarian

acrobat	waitress	gardener	stunt pilot
actor	court reporter	garbage man	nurse
ballet dancer	jailer	real estate agent	nun
banjo player	sheriff	physicist	diamond merchant
clown	night watchman	chemist	bicycle racer
lion tamer	sailor	engineer	timekeeper
violinist	biologist	demolitions expert	child psychologist
emperor	nanny	rocket engineer	optometrist
mayor	bill collector	astronaut	prime minister
president	bodyguard	bus driver	ambassador
dishwasher	bridal consultant	jet pilot	judge

mother	the flirt	the grouch	the veteran
father	the hustler	the hothead	the warrior
aunt	the diplomat	the go-getter	the winner
uncle	the lazy one	the giver	the loser
cousin	the slow one	the outcast	
twin	the fast one	the organizer	
the protector	the bore	the prisoner	
the preacher	the busybody	the psycho	
the nobody	the believer	the rascal	
the loner	the avenger	the snob	
the know-it-all	the amateur	the traitor	

SHUFFLE A CHARACTER

Your teacher has given you two cards, each with a job or a role on it. Choose the job or role on one of the cards to help you create a fictional character. Then complete the items below. Remember, you are the person creating the character, so there are no wrong answers. Now is the time to use your imagination!

1.   My character's job or role: _____

2.   One weird or specific detail about my character: _____
_____
(Use the list below for ideas. Feel free to use ideas not on the list, instead.)

Loves baked potatoes	**Wears only blue**	**Owns a monkey**
Wears rings on every toe	**Plays goalie on a soccer team**	**Always walks on tiptoe**
Loves tigers	**Sings like a lark**	**Can do a back handspring**
Is scared of the light	**Is learning to be funny**	**Loves the library**
Is allergic to armadillos	**Always wears gloves**	**Has very, very dry hands**
Always wears three necklaces	**Likes to play cards**	**Loves peppermint candy**
Always carries a $100 bill	**Is clumsy**	**Collects beetles**
Always wears sandals	**Raises chickens**	**Likes to draw cars**
Is learning to eat broccoli	**Plays a drum**	**Wears a Superman cape to school**
Wears red nail polish	**Writes books**	
Always wears a baseball cap	**Drives a 16-wheeler truck**	**Always whispers**
Wears hair braided	**Makes diamond jewelry**	**Loves the desert**
Has cat-eye contact lenses	**Takes digital photos**	**Watches birds**
Steals gum	**Builds church organs**	**Makes quilts**
Eats pencil erasers	**Hates to play video games**	**Can't change a tire**
Drinks coffee all day	**Likes to hike**	**Collects umbrellas**
Is a vegetarian	**Races BMX bicycles**	**His/her grandfather recently died**
Doesn't own a cell phone	**Builds race cars**	
Likes to burn candles	**Collects stamps**	**Likes to sweep and mop floors**
Hates chocolate chip cookies	**Drives a Jaguar**	**Is a werewolf**
Is allergic to peanuts	**Plays accordion**	**Eats turtle soup every Monday**

3.   Name (first, middle, last, and perhaps nickname): _____

4.   Male or female? _____

5.   One thing this character wants is: _____
_____

6.   One thing this character fears is: _____
_____

7.   Write a paragraph describing your character. (Use your own paper.)
_____

YOU CAN'T HAVE THAT! and WHAT ARE YOU AFRAID OF?
Creating conflict

Overview. This activity helps students learn a simple way to create conflict for a story by looking at what a character wants or fears.

Getting started. Introduce students to the idea that conflict is central to a story. Conflict always involves a struggle of some kind, based on a problem.

A good way to find conflict is to look at what the main character wants or fears. When a character has trouble getting what he or she wants or has to face a fear, a struggle of some kind develops, even if the struggle is within the character.

Ask students to look at the characters they created in the "Shuffle a Character" activity. They were asked to fill in two questions:

- "One thing this character wants is _____."
- "One thing this character fears is_____."

Ask students to think about *why* their character can't have what he or she wants. What conflict or struggle could develop from the character trying to get it? The story might be based on the struggle to solve that problem.

Or if the character is afraid of something, how could that fear lead to a problem? The story might be based on having the character deal with that fear.

Example based on a want: Jennifer Fellows collects umbrellas. She wants the rare umbrella used by the nanny in the movie, *Mary Poppins.*

Why can't she have it? Maybe she doesn't know where the umbrella is. Maybe the man who owns it won't sell it to her. Maybe he will, but she doesn't have nearly enough money. The story might be about how she struggles to solve any of these problems.

Example based on a fear: Irene Bernallio is afraid of heights. How does her fear lead to a problem? Maybe her friends all decide to go hiking, but something goes wrong and Irene winds up being the only one who can rescue a friend. The story could be about how she overcomes her fear of heights in order to save a life.

Or maybe her fear is discovered by a bully, and he uses that fear to torment her. The story could be about how she has to learn to overcome her fear of heights so that the bully no longer has any power over her.

Have students come up with possible problems for each want and fear listed in "You Can't Have That!" and "What Are You Afraid Of?"

YOU CAN'T HAVE THAT!

STUDENT INSTRUCTIONS

One thing a story needs is conflict. Conflict always involves a struggle of some kind, based on a problem.

One good way to find conflict is to look at what the main character wants, and why. What problems might be caused if the person can't have what he or she wants? What happens if he or she tries to get it? What struggle or conflict might develop?

The column on the left, below, shows some characters and what they want. Imagine that you are writing a story about these characters. What possible story problem might develop? What conflict might develop? Fill in the chart with your ideas. The first item is done for you, as an example.

What a character wants, and why	Possible story problems	Conflict (struggle) that might develop
Frank wants a bike so that he doesn't have to walk to school or ride the bus.	He doesn't have the money to buy a bike.	Frank wants to get a job to earn the money, but his parents won't allow it.
Jill wants to go to the movies tonight so she can see Justin, a guy she likes.		
Peter wants to make an A in history class so that he can please his father.		
Liz wants to sneak into an abandoned house to see if it's really haunted.		
Mario wants to go out for football because he loves it and is good at it.		

WHAT ARE YOU AFRAID OF?

As you know, one thing a story needs is conflict. Conflict always involves a struggle of some kind, based on a problem.

   You have already learned that one good way to find conflict is to look at what the main character wants. Another way is to look at what the character fears. What problems might develop because of this fear? What happens when the character tries to avoid what he or she fears?

   The column on the left, below, shows some characters and what they fear. Imagine that you are writing a story about these characters. What possible story problem might develop? What conflict might develop? Fill in the chart with your ideas. The first item is done for you, as an example.

What a character fears, and why	Possible story problem	Conflict (struggle) that might develop
Jill fears the dark because she is afraid of what might lurk there.	She won't go anywhere after dark unless someone is with her.	Her brothers and sisters are tired of having to go with her everywhere and refuse to do it anymore.
Franklin fears eating peanuts because he is allergic to them.		
Mr. Miller fears having anyone find out that he can't read because he would be humiliated.		
Merry fears learning to ski because she is so afraid of falling.		
Jamal fears what his friends will think when they find out he is taking dance lessons.		

NICE TO MEET YOU
Creating characters and conflict for an original story

Overview. With the previous exercises, students learned some techniques for creating believable characters and conflict. Now they begin writing an original story of their own. With "Nice to Meet You," they create the main characters and conflict for their own story.

Getting started. Talk with students about how they will now begin creating a story of their own. Pass out "Nice to Meet You." Go over it with students, emphasizing that they will pull together all the techniques they have learned for creating characters. Now they will create characters who are all involved in some way in the same story.

Explain that "Nice to Meet You" will help them create the main character and conflict, as well as two other characters. They may, of course, add fewer characters or more characters. The chart is meant only as a guideline to help them plan.

NICE TO MEET YOU

STUDENT INSTRUCTIONS

Now it's time to start a story of your own. The best place to begin is with your main characters and the main conflict. Complete the charts below to help you do the first part of your planning.

MAIN CHARACTER

Name	Job or role	(Optional) Second job or role	One weird thing or specific detail

Choose A or B below

	What the character wants, and why	Possible story problem	Conflict (struggle) that might develop
A			

	What the character fears, and why	Possible story problem	Conflict (struggle) that might develop
B			

OTHER CHARACTERS

Name	Job or role	(Optional) Second job or role	One weird thing or specific detail

THINKING MEAN
Developing the plot

Overview. After students have decided on the main characters and conflict for their story, they must make it hard for the character to either (a) get what he or she wants, or (b) avoid what he or she fears.

When a story event makes the situation worse for a character by increasing the conflict, it's called a complication. A good plot makes things increasingly difficult for a character. This means that writers can't be nice to their characters; they *must* make things worse for them at every turn, until the ending.

This activity helps students think of story complications to develop a plot.

Getting started. With your class, read over the instructions for the "Thinking Mean" activity. Using the main character and conflict developed in "Nice to Meet You," students will think of 3-5 five things that could go wrong for the main character and rank these complications. (If students write the events on index cards, they can easily move them around and play with the order.)

THINKING MEAN

When you create interesting characters, you may like them so much that you want to make things easy for them. That's a mistake. Story characters must face hard things, or the story is boring. When you create the plot for a story, you must be mean to the characters, making it hard for them to get what they want or hard to avoid what they fear.

And what is the plot of the story? It is the plan of action. It is what happens. A good plot makes things increasingly difficult for a character. The tricky part is to remember that, at the end, the character must be able to deal with the problem somehow, either successfully or unsuccessfully.

A fairly easy way to start developing a plot is to follow the steps below.

1. First, describe your character and the character's want or fear. _____

    _____

    _____

2. What is the problem caused by this want or fear? _____

    _____

    _____

3. Now be mean to your character. What are five complications or things that could go wrong for the character? The complications should be related to the character's main problem.

    _____A. _____

    _____

    _____B. _____

    _____

    _____C _____

    _____

    _____D. _____

    _____

    _____E. _____

    _____

THINKING MEAN, *continued*

STUDENT INSTRUCTIONS

4. Decide on the order of events. On the blanks in front of each complication, rank the complications. Put a "1" beside the easiest complication and a "5" beside the hardest complication. Then rank the others in between.

5. Plan a solution. Decide if the character solves the problem. For a happy ending, he or she will. For a sad ending, he or she will not.

    •   Will your character successfully overcome the story conflict? (In other words, will the character get what he or she wants or overcome his or her fears?)

        _____Yes _____No

    •   If "yes," explain *how* the character will solve the problem and overcome the story conflict.

        _____

        _____

        _____

    •   If "no," explain why the character can't solve the conflict. What will happen instead? What is the last thing that will happen in the story? _____

        _____

        _____

WHERE AM I?

Practice creating interesting settings

Overview. After characters and plot, setting is an important element to plan before writing a story. "Where Am I?" uses the "Sensory Word Bank" activity sheet (page 28) but extends it to fit a new purpose, that of making the setting come alive.

This exercise is used before students create the setting for the story they have started in the previous exercises.

Getting started. Discuss with your students what a setting is and why it is important to a story. A setting can include the historical time period, time of day, climate, weather, buildings, roads, etc.

Each element limits what type of story can be told. A story set in the time of cavemen will be very different from a story set in medieval Europe. Stories set near the Egyptian pyramids will be vastly different from those set in the Siberian tundra.

"Where Am I?" asks students to create a description of a place without using key words that are closely associated with the place. To do so, they must take the time to think about what the setting is really like.

Hand out the student instructions for "Where Am I?" and also a "Sensory Word Bank" activity sheet. Read through the instructions with the students. Have them choose one setting to describe and then complete a "Sensory Word Bank" activity sheet for that setting before they begin writing. The word bank will help them come up with words and phrases to use in the description of their setting.

After students have written their descriptions, read some aloud and let students guess what setting is described.

Going further. Let students choose their own setting to describe. Remind them to leave out key words and let the descriptions evoke the setting. Read aloud some of the descriptions and ask students to guess, "Where Am I?"

WHERE AM I?

The setting of a story is where and when the story takes place. Does it take place in the future? In the past? Today? Where is the story taking place? Is it on a ship in the ocean? In an urban penthouse? In a barn on a farm? The setting has a big effect on what can happen in a story.

Choose one of the settings below and write a one paragraph description, but without using the words in italics. Think about the setting and what it would be like to be in this place. Before you start writing, complete a "Sensory Word Bank" activity sheet, applying the five senses to the setting you have chosen.

End your description with the words, "Where Am I?"

1. Circus
   Words you can't use: *circus, clown, big top, ringmaster, rings, trapeze, tightrope, elephant.*

2. Grocery store
   Words you can't use: *food, cans, fruits, vegetables, cereal, milk, basket, cart, candy, Coke.*

3. Football game
   Words you can't use: *football, game, field, quarterback, center, halfback, fullback, tight end, hike, hut, play.*

4. Birthday party
   Words you can't use: *cake, candles, gifts, "how old," party, happy, birthday, presents, balloons.*

5. Mall
   Words you can't use: *mall, store, names of specific stores or restaurants, hang out, stroll, friends.*

Setting Choice: _____

_____

_____

_____

_____

_____

_____

_____

_____

_____

WHAT'S MY MOOD?
Using setting to create mood

Overview. Details about the setting can be used to create a mood for a story. For this activity, students will be asked to choose appropriate details to support a certain mood. First they will complete a "Sensory Word Bank" activity sheet, page 28. Then they will write a paragraph creating the mood through a description of a setting.

This exercise is for practice, before students create a setting and mood for the story they have been working on with the previous exercises.

Getting started. With your class, review the "Sensory Word Bank" activity sheet. Ask students to suggest words or phrases for each sense to describe a *happy* playground. Record these on the board for everyone to see. Then ask the students to suggest words or phrases for each sense to describe a *scary* playground.

Examples for a happy playground:

See: *red slide, blue swings*
Hear: *laughter, giggles of girls*
Feel: *warm sunshine on faces*
Taste: *chocolate bars pulled from pockets*
Smell: *the scent of chocolate chip cookies wafting from the cafeteria window and spreading over the playground*

Examples for a scary playground:

See: *swing hanging from a broken, rusty chain*
Hear: *high-pitched squeal of terror*
Feel: *scalding hot slide*
Taste: *nearly black banana*
Smell: *rotten egg smell from trash cans*

Discuss. Discuss how the choice of sensory details can change the emotional feeling or mood of a setting. A description can help show a character's mood without explaining it.

For example, a simple description of a tree outside a man's house might do nothing to help set a joyous mood, if it is written like this:

The tall oak stood beside his house. He passed it every day when he walked out to get in his car. The ground crunched with dead leaves. Looking up, he saw a bird's nest in the top branches.

But what if the tree description helped set the mood? Imagine that the story is about a man on his way to the hospital to see his wife who has cancer. The description might help show his mood so that we understand it without having it explained.

Nestled in the crook of the topmost branches, the nest swayed. A feather fluttered out, caught in the wind and spun upward. It stuck on a bare branch, hesitated, and then the wind caught it again. This time it floated down through the naked branches. Down. Rough bark caught at it, but it kept falling anyway. It landed at his feet. He knelt and picked it up. It was a blue jay feather, as blue as Amelia's eyes. He craned his neck toward the nest and wished somehow that he could put the feather back where it belonged.

Pass out the "What's My Mood?" activity. Read the directions together and ask students to complete the activity.

WHAT'S MY MOOD?

How do you create a certain mood with a story? How can you make it feel scary or funny or sad, for example? One way is with the words you use to describe the setting.

1. Choose a setting and a mood that might be used for a story. Here are some examples of settings and moods. You may use any of these or think of others on your own:

Settings	Moods
basketball game	scary
dinner table	angry
library	happy
ice cream shop	sad
gymnasium	lonely
classroom	worried
parade	excited
zoo	mysterious
cave	funny

My choice for setting _____

My choice for mood _____

2. Write the setting and mood you have chosen at the top of your "Sensory Word Bank" activity sheet. Then complete the Word Bank, thinking of sensory details that support the mood you have chosen. As always, try to write at least three details for each sense.

3. Choose details from your word bank and write a paragraph using the details to describe the setting and create a mood. End with these words: "What's my mood?"

4. Read your paragraph aloud to your class or group and let others guess what mood you tried to create.

WRITING YOUR STORY
Putting it all together

Overview. Now students have practiced creating characters, conflict, plot, setting, and mood. It's time for them to pull everything together into a basic outline and, finally, to write an original story. You may have students continue with the characters created in the exercises on pages 69 to 74. They simply need to add "setting" and "mood," and they will have the basic outline for their story.

Getting started. Pass out "Writing Your Story." Have students fill in the blanks, using the character and conflict they created in earlier exercises.

They will need to decide on a setting and a mood for their story now. Those are the last two details of their basic outline.

Finally, ask students to write the first draft of their story. They should introduce their main character and the story conflict, followed by the complications the character must face. Finally, students write the solution or the last thing that happens.

WRITING YOUR STORY

Check your story. By now, you should be able to fill in these blanks:

This will be a story about the character _____, who

wants or fears _____

_____.

However, the character has this main problem: _____

_____.

And the character is involved in this conflict or struggle:_____

_____.

The following complications happen to the main character, from easiest to hardest:

1 _____

2 _____

3. _____

4. (optional)_____

5. (optional)_____

Finally, at the end of the story, this happens: _____

_____

The setting: _____

_____

The mood: _____

_____

Finally, it's time to write your story! Start by introducing your character and the main story conflict. Then the character must face the complications. Finally, write the solution or the last thing that happens in the story.

ZOOM AND PAN
Ins and outs of settings

Overview. You may want to have your students experiment further with setting, before or after they write their first stories. "Zoom and Pan" has them look at setting in a different way.

When taking pictures, photographers must decide how close they want the camera to get to the subject. The same idea is important in writing. Do you want a close-up or do you want to show the background? "Zoom and Pan" gives students practice creating both zoom and panoramic views.

Getting started. With your class, discuss the differences between a zoom and a panorama. A zoom takes a small thing and blows it up so that it fills the entire picture. A panorama shows the big picture, including the background and setting.

If you write a zoom view of a football game, you might focus on the huddle of players on the ten-yard line. The quarterback limps over, favoring his right leg. The center wipes mud from the football onto his silver pants, while the linebacker scratches a mosquito bite on his neck. The players' shabby shoes tell of how hard they have worked this season to be in the finals.

If you write a panorama of a football game, you might describe the setting as if you were sitting at the top of the bleachers. Spread below you is the striped field with red uniforms dominating one side and blue uniforms the other. The parking lot is full, with yellow school buses parked near the stadium's entrance. Cheerleaders jump and yell in front of each stand, while uniformed band members line up along the sideline, waiting for their cue to march onto the field.

Example. Here's an example of both panorama and zoom setting descriptions from the same book of fiction, *The Wayfinder*. (See "Bibliography", page 107.) Winchal, the main character, is climbing down a cliff into the Rift, a deep canyon.

Zoom: (p. 62)

He turned toward the cliff and hung his feet over until he felt the ledge. It was only eight or ten inches wide. He started creeping sideways, and downward, until his head was below the top of the cliff. He made himself look at the rock face and not out into the open canyon. The rock was yellow ocher streaked with browns and reds. From a distance the rock face looked bare, but small grasses and shrubs had found occasional footholds and grew clinging to the sides of the Rift. Patches of moss, nurtured by the mists that rose from the Rift during the wet season, were dry and crumbly now.

Panorama: (p. 64)

Win had descended perhaps a fourth of the way, and the Rift bottom was taking on a new look as he got closer. The cliff face shimmered ocher and russet in the heat. The silvery blue river appeared larger as it meandered through lush forests. Birds soared below him, sometimes spiraling down to the treetops below. The air was brilliantly clear, and his spirits lifted.

After discussion, pass out "Zoom and Pan" and also two "Sensory Detail Word Bank" activity sheets. (If students are familiar enough with "Sensory Word Bank" activity sheets by now, they can simply create their own, using their own paper.)

ZOOM AND PAN

STUDENT INSTRUCTIONS

When you are trying to describe a setting, it is important to decide how you want to look at the scene. Do you want to be standing far away, looking at an overall picture? Or do you want to stand very close and see lots of details?

A zoom takes a small thing and blows it up so it fills the entire picture. Think of standing next to the quarterback in the huddle and watching the faces of the other football players as the play is called.

A panorama shows the big picture, including the background and setting. Think of sitting at the top of the bleachers and describing a football field spread out in front of you.

1. Choose one of the settings below. (Or use your own idea for a setting.)

your bedroom	your mother's office	a city on another planet
your best friend's bedroom	your father's office	the moon
our sister or brother's bedroom	a city park	a scientist's laboratory
a swimming pool	a barnyard	the emergency room
a football game	your favorite store	a locker room
an English classroom	a motor boat	inside a limousine
a science classroom	a horse stable	at the zoo
a gymnasium	a favorite fishing place	an attic
a basketball game	downtown	a dark basement
a forest	a battle	a favorite restaurant
a circus	a castle	on a sailboat
a kitchen	an elegant ball	in an airplane

My choice of setting _____

2. Create a "Sensory Detail Word Bank" for a *zoom* description of your setting.

3. Write a description of your setting from a *zoom* viewpoint.

4. Create a "Sensory Word Bank" for a *panoramic* description of your setting.

5. Write a description of your setting from a *panoramic* viewpoint.

FOLK
TALES
■ ■ ■

One kind of fiction students enjoy writing is the folk tale. This section focuses on a folk tale that is particularly fun to write—the one involving a character known as the Fool.

FOLK TALES
Background reading

Overview. Before students try to write in the folk tale tradition, they should start by reading a variety of these tales. One variety is variously called the Simpleton, the Noodlehead, the Silly, or the Fool folk tale. In these folk tales, the main character has no common sense, and the plot revolves around the nonsensical choices he or she makes. This is the kind of tale students will focus on for the next several activities.

Getting started. Collect several examples of folk tales with the Fool as the main character. Look for folk tale collections with these well-known Fools: Clever Elsie (German), Fearless Simpleton (Italian), Goha the Simple (Arabic), Simple Ivanushka (Russian). Isaac Bashevis Singer has collected and retold several Yiddish tales of Fools in his Newbery Honor book, *Zlateh the Goat and Other Stories.* (See "Bibliography," page 107.)

Read several stories with the class.

Discussion. After students have read several folk tales, discuss what a folk tale really is: a story that has been passed down by telling it to others. Here are several characteristics of folk tales:

- a ritual opening (such as "Once upon a time")
- a ritual closing (such as "And they lived happily ever after")
- traditional or stereotypical characters without a lot of character development
- a story line that jumps straight into the action without much background
- exaggerated silliness
- things often occurring in a series of three (such as in "The Three Little Pigs" or "Goldilocks and the Three Bears")
- often teaches a lesson

Discuss the types of mistakes the Fools make in the stories you read with the students. Why are they considered fools?

FOOLS AND NOODLEHEADS
Writing folk tales

Overview. Students will read and discuss a folk tale involving a Fool and then write their own folk tale featuring a Fool.

Background. Read together with the students the following book: *Epossumondas.* (See bibliography, page 107.) In the story, the Fool, Epossumondas, tries to figure out how to carry home things that his auntie gives him.

Discuss. Ask students to list the problems that Epossumondas tries to solve. (He decides how to carry various things home. He carries cake by squashing it in his hands, butter by putting it on his head under a hat, a puppy by cooling it off in water and wrapping it in leaves, bread by dragging it home with a string.)

Then have students think of ways a Fool like Epossumondas might solve other problems.

Examples:
1. How to stay warm:
   - Build a wall around a city to keep the cold out.
   - Open the door to let the sun shine in.
   - Catch the sun's reflection in the water and bring it into the house.

2. How to travel to a city:
   - Try to push a mountain out of the way.
   - Try to move the river bed.
   - Try to catch a bird and let it fly you.

3. How to fix a broken computer.
   - Unplug it and let it sleep for a while.
   - Bring a working computer and set beside the broken computer and hope that the working computer's good habits will rub off on the other one.
   - Blow on it with a hair dryer to warm it up.

Getting started. With your class, review the instructions on the "Fools and Noodleheads" activity. Students should fill in the form with names of characters, problem to be solved, and suggested ways to solve the problem. They will also decide on a ritual opening and closing. After the form is filled out, they should write their original folk tale.

FOOLS AND NOODLEHEADS

You have read some folk tales that feature a character known as the Fool, the Noodlehead, the Simpleton, and other names. Now it's time to write a folk tale involving the Fool. First, plan your tale by completing the following:

Ritual opening. Choose a ritual opening for your story. You might try one of these:

Once upon a time…
Once there was and once there was not…
Long, long ago…
Let's tell another story…
In a faraway land…
There once…
Many years ago…
Did you ever hear the story of…

Ritual opening _____

Traditional characters. Use names that tell the role of the traditional characters. Example: Simple Simon, Wise Gertie.

Name of Fool: _____

Name of Smart One: _____

Problem to be solved. Usually, the fool has to solve the problem of how to do an ordinary daily task. Choose a problem for your fool to solve. Here are some ideas:

- **How to toast bread**
- **How to make a snowman**
- **How to carry a pet to the vet**
- **How to take a picture**
- **How to paint fingernails**

- **How to mow the grass**
- **How to clean a room**
- **How to bathe a dog**
- **How to build a fire**
- **How to sharpen a pencil**

- **How to eat an orange**
- **How to rake leaves**
- **How to prepare a bowl of cereal**

Problem to be solved in your story: _____

(continued)

FOOLS AND NOODLEHEADS, *continued*

Exaggeration. Folk tales often exaggerate the events that happen. Decide on foolish ways to solve the problem. Think about how exaggeration can make this part funnier or more interesting.

Exaggeration in your story:

1. _____

2. _____

3. _____

Ritual closing. Choose a ritual ending for your story. You might try one of these:

And they lived happily ever after.
Time never ends.
And so they achieved their hearts desire.
It all happened a long time ago and it's all true.
And, as far as anyone knows, they are still…
But that is another story…

The ritual closing in your story:

_____

Write. Use these two pages as your outline as you write your folk tale.

Paper Lightning • Copyright © 2008 by Darcy Pattison • Cottonwood Press, Inc. • 800-864-4297 • www.cottonwoodpress.com

SAMPLE
ANSWERS
. . .

Billions-and-Billions to One-and-Only-One, pages 15-16

1. Billions-and-billions noun: *shoes*
   More specific: *Nikes*
   One-and-only-one description: *battered Nikes with all the tread worn off and a hole in each toe*

2. Billions-and-billions noun: *bread*
   More specific: *rye toast*
   One-and-only-one description: *warm rye toast drenched in butter and homemade apple butter*

3. Billions-and-billions noun: *color*
   More specific: *magenta*
   One-and-only-one description: *a bright magenta that looked like cooked cranberries*

4. Billions-and-billions noun: *bird*
   More specific: *parrot*
   One-and-only-one description: *a lime green parrot with a loud, raspy scream and a dislike of little children*

5. Billions-and-billions noun: *truck*
   More specific: *18 wheeler*
   One-and-only-one description: *a crushed 18 wheeler that had slid off a steep embankment*

6. Billions-and-billions noun: *building*
   More specific: *skyscraper*
   One-and-only-one description: *a gleaming new skyscraper that towered over the old brick buildings surrounding it*

7. Billions-and-billions noun: *pencil*
   More specific: *#2 pencil*
   One-and-only-one description: *a stub of a #2 pencil full of tooth marks*

8. Billions-and-billions noun: *cloth*
   More specific: *silk*
   One-and-only-one description: *exotic, imported Chinese silk with golden threads and scarlet fringe*

9. Billions-and-billions noun: *pants*
   More specific: *jodhpurs*
   One-and-only-one description: *black silk jodhpurs worn by the Kentucky Derby winning jockey*

10. Billions-and-billions noun: *machine*
    More specific: *copier*
    One-and-only-one description: *a color copier that prints 100 double-sided sheets per minute and also collates and staples*

Getting Rid of "Nothing" Adjectives, page 18

1. Hunter and Cal went to a **popular** restaurant with his friends to celebrate his birthday.
2. For lunch, they ate **steaming, spicy** chili.
3. After lunch, the waiter carried out a **towering fudge** cake.
4. Everyone thought the cake was **moist** and **delicious.**
5. His friends sang "Happy Birthday." Their voices were **off-key,** and everyone laughed.

Hunter took home his **thoughtful** and **expensive** presents.

Getting Rid of "Nothing" Verbs, page 20

1. With a silly, cartoon-mouse voice, the clown **squeaked** out a song.
2. Its hooves **pounded** the earth as the horse took the lead.
3. Inside the circus tent, a woman **vomited** and then **fainted**.
4. Elephants constantly **grab** food and **stuff** it in their mouths.
5. The circus band **blasted** away in the center of the arena.

The trapeze artists' costumes **sparkle** high above the crowd.

Getting Rid of "Nothing" Adverbs, page 21

1. At the dog show, the judges **painstakingly examined** every dog.
2. The German shepherd **lumbered lazily** around the ring.
3. The Dalmation **leaped lightly** onto the chair.
4. After waking up, the golden retriever **scrambled** to his food dish and **inhaled** every morsel.
5. Sitting on a girl's lap, the Chihuahua **snored softly.**

The crowd **clapped wildly** when the bloodhound **pranced** into the ring.

Sensory Details, page 25

David wandered down the musty hallway toward the hotel lobby. What secrets did this old place hide behind each door? David wanted to open every one. He stopped at the last door, a turquoise blue one. A dull brass number read "1." He listened. Silence. He put a hand on the doorknob, but couldn't make himself turn it. Quickly, he turned away, and winced as the floor squeaked. No reaction from anywhere.

Silence, again. This was the quietest place he'd ever been, except for a church. Somewhere in the hotel, food was cooking, spreading a spicy aroma that made David's stomach growl. He had no idea where to find either his father or the food. His earlier anger returned and he clenched his fists: why had Father left him alone in this strange place?

Sensory Word Bank, pages 27-28

Topic: an exciting moment at a sports event (The home football team intercepts the ball with 20 seconds left and scores the winning touchdown)

- Hear: The hush of the crowd. The roar of the crowd. Band music. People yelling, clapping and cheering. The announcer shouting, "Touchdown!"
- See: The quarterback throwing the football. The football being intercepted. The player who intercepted the football running for a touchdown. Fans standing. The player making a touchdown. The referee signaling a touchdown.
- Smell: Popcorn, pizza, nacho cheese sauce, perfume from a woman who put on too much.
- Taste: Popcorn, pizza, nacho cheese sauce and chips, soda, water, candy.
- Feel: The hard bleachers, the hug of my friend when we won, the cool fall air on my face.

Packed with Facts #1, page 30

The Gold State Coach

Like Atlas's corded and muscled back,

King George's coach was simply colossal.

Twenty-four feet in length and thirteen high,

Eight-foot three-inches wide: it weighed four tons.

The coach's framework was made of eight palm trees

Which branched to support the roof. At each corner

A lion's head proclaimed British triumphs.

Three cherubs on top represented England,

Scotland, Ireland; the three together

Supported the Royal Crown. The coach's body

Was leather-slung between four gold sea-gods;

Massive wheels bore this Monarch of Oceans.

Painted, gilded, ornate, and triumphal–

George's royal coach was simply superb.

From the royal stables at Hampton Court,

came buff-colored Hanoverian creams:

pale manes and tails, they stood seventeen hands.

Though jostled through the noisy, crowded streets,

Eight strong, they pulled the massive coach with calm

and steady treads. With pageantry, King George

rode proud. And when the Empire's weight and wealth

passed by, even the very earth trembled.

Packed with Facts #2, page 31

The Buffalo River

One day, I put on an orange life preserver and stepped into an aluminum canoe to float the Buffalo River, a 132-mile river that winds through the Ozark Mountains of Arkansas. In 1972, Congress named it our first National River.

The river was wide and slow moving. Through clear depths, I spied small-mouth bass feeding. Several red-eared sliders, which were sunning on a fallen log, slipped into the water. Coming around a limestone bluff, I surprised great blue herons, which took off in a whir of wings. The sun didn't bother me most of the time because the canoe glided in and out of the shade of oak and hickory branches. Squirrels chattered at me; chickadees and tit-mouse birds scolded me. Black snakes, which were basking on overhanging limbs, slid off into the water when I came close.

Packed with Facts Word Bank, pages 33-34

Topic: The Taj Mahal

Statistics	Facts	Proper nouns (and how they relate to the topic)
Completed around 1648	Located in India	India (country where the Taj Mahal is located)
Over 1000 elephants used during construction	Very large	Agra (city in India where the Taj Mahal is located)
Attracts 2-3 million visitors per year	One of the 7 wonders of the world	Shah Jahan (Emperor who ruled when the Taj Mahal was built)
Base is 55 meters on each side	mausoleum	Mumtaz Mahal (wife of Shah Jahan. Taj built for her)
large dome – 35 meters high	made of white marble	Ismail Afandi (designed main dome)
finial on large dome made of gold until early 1800s	inlaid with semi-precious stones	Taj (nickname)
4 large minarets surrounding main dome each more than 40 meters tall	designated a UNESCO World Heritage Site	Amanat Khan (chief calligrapher for the Taj)
garden surrounding Taj is 300 meters square	Most popular tourist attraction in India	Mughal (the Taj's style of architecture)

Ugly Writing #1, page 38

Road Whiz strutted regally into the back yard, with her head held high, like she was balancing a crown. Her long pointed muzzle lifted to sniff.

Across the fifteen feet of lawn, the yellow rose bushes basked in the brilliant July sun. I sniffed, too. It had been a while since I noticed that sweet rose smell. Whiz tugged at her red leash and her claws clicked on the brick patio.

Mom would kill me if I let Whiz tear up her flowers. Worried, I stroked Whiz's soft ears. Greyhounds needed to run, though, so what could I do? I would have to run with her.

Click. I unsnapped the leash from Whiz's collar.

For speed, a greyhound's long, muscular legs depend on the lungs housed in the wide chest. This time, though, Whiz's chest didn't expand at all before she bounded away, floating over the springy grass. But when I followed, the grass tugged at me. I stumbled and wind-milled my arms to keep from falling. The gap between Whiz and myself lengthened to two feet, five feet, twelve feet. Whiz hit the path at a lope, kicking up puffs of soft dirt.

My heart pounded in my ears. So far, she was on the path, leaving the roses alone. "Whiz! Come here, girl!"

Whiz circled a tree, then stretched out her legs, reaching for the ground so she could push off and tuck back up like a coiled spring, ready to reach and push off again. Her grace was punctuated by gentle thumps. Then, she veered off and slowed.

Whiz's black nose touched a drooping rose. Petals from Mom's award-winning yellow rose bush drifted to the ground. And before I could lunge for her collar, Whiz hiked a leg and marked the rose bush as her territory.

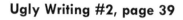

Ugly Writing #2, page 39

Tiny |alpine| flowers covered the <u>meadow</u> in (drifts of yellow) I was so enchanted, I forgot to watch where I was stepping. Even though it was the middle of June, piles of (dirty snow) still lay in the deep shadows. Of course, I stepped into snow that was |three inches| deeper than my hiking boots. I <u>peeled</u> off my (red) mittens, then <u>bent</u> and <u>flicked</u> the (icy snow) out of the boot but it was too late. The top of my sock was |suddenly| (cold and wet,) like my fingers. I <u>kicked</u> at the snow drift in irritation.

A |sudden| thunder (crack) startled me, and I <u>jerked</u> back under the pines. My boots <u>crushed</u> the low boughs, releasing the |tangy| (pine smell.) (Lightning strobed) through the clouds. I <u>groaned.</u> If only I'd brought the map out of the van's glove box. If only I had my compass. Instead, I was lost at |12,000 feet| elevation and had no idea what direction I was traveling or what direction would take me back down to the van. Lost. Could it get any worse?

Yes.

A white <u>marble</u> rolled toward the toe of my hiking boot. No, not a marble.

A (clattering) made me look up. Something <u>smacked</u> my forehead, (stinging) hard and bringing tears to my eyes. Hail. I (threw my hands) up to cover my face, <u>crouched</u> and backed into a |thick| pine. Snow <u>spilled</u> from the boughs into my hair and face, spreading (fingers of cold) until I was <u>shivering</u> in spite of my (red wool sweater.) My boots filled with more (damp snow) and water <u>seeped</u> down my ankle until my socks were (totally soaked.) But I didn't care. I put my back against the (rough bark,) held aside the |prickly| <u>pine needles</u> and watched the storm in wonder. My previous irritation was swept aside, replaced by a |crazy| exhilaration. The (patter of hailstones) grew to a dull (roar) as the sky <u>hurled</u> (hard icy balls) until four inches of <u>hailstones</u> <u>suffocated</u> the alpine flowers.

Sorting Skunks, pages 47-48

Appearance:

1. Skunks weigh about 10 pounds.
2. They are about two feet long.

Skunks' habits:

1. They are more active at night

Skunks food habits:

1. Skunks eat insects, fruits, and berries.
2. They locate food more by smell than by sight.

3. They will tear into garbage bags and eat what they find.

Sorting Hummingbirds, pages 49-50

Size:

1. Hummingbirds weigh 1/100 of an ounce
2. They are four inches long.
3. They have a wingspan of about six inches.
4. They need to eat twice their body weight in food each day.

Sorting Hummingbirds, continued.

Strength:

1. They fly south to Central America for the winter.
2. When they migrate, they cross 600 miles of the Gulf of Mexico.
3. When they migrate, they fly more than 1850 miles.

Dangers:

1. They are so small that other animals eat them.
2. They have been caught and eaten by frogs.
3. They have been caught and eaten by dragonflies.
4. They have been caught and eaten by praying mantises.
5. They can get caught in spider webs.

Sorting Chewing Gum, pages 51-52

Positive things about chewing gum:

1. It is easy to carry around.
2. It can help whiten your teeth.
3. It can keep your breath fresh.
4. It can help your teeth stay healthy.

The gum base

1. All chewing gum has a gum base.
2. The gum base is the part that is not dissolved during chewing.

Flavors

1. To the gum base, manufacturers add flavors.
2. Flavors may have 10-100 chemicals.
3. Spearmint flavoring comes from a plant.
4. Peppermint flavoring comes from a plant.

Miscellaneous ingredients

1. To the gum base, manufacturers add texture.
2. To the gum base, manufacturers add colors.

Sweeteners

1. To the gum base, manufacturers add sweeteners.
2. Sweeteners are the main ingredient in chewing gum.
3. Sweeteners make the gum bulky and big.

(Left out: Sometimes gum gets a crunchy outer layer.)

What Is My Opinion? page 58-59

1. Topic: Using a cell phone while driving is bad.
2. Improved version: Using a cell phone while driving should be illegal.
3. Reasons why someone might agree:

   Talking on the phone while driving is dangerous because the driver's mind is on the conversation, not on the road.

   Someone could get bad news on a cell phone, get upset, and cause an accident.

   Many lives are at stake when a person is behind the steering wheel of a vehicle, and the person should concentrate on driving that vehicle, for the safety of all.

4. Reasons why someone might disagree:

   The government shouldn't be able to tell us what to do if we aren't harming anyone.

   It is our right to call anyone we want at any time.

   Many phone calls involve emergencies, and drivers should be able to answer at any time.

   Talking on a cell phone while driving is no different than eating or listening to the radio while driving. It is possible to do two things at once.

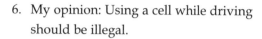

6. My opinion: Using a cell while driving should be illegal.

   Reasons:

   1. Multi-tasking while driving is dangerous.

   2. Drivers who talk on cell phones are endangering others.

   3. Driving requires a person's complete attention.

Making Reasons Believable, page 61-62

My opinion: Using a cell phone while driving is bad.

Reasons:

1. Multi-tasking while driving is dangerous.

   Support: According to CarAccident.com, 26% of all traffic fatalities are caused by distracted drivers.

2. Drivers who talk on cell phones are endangering others.

   Support: CarAccident.com also reports that traffic fatalities caused by cell phone users have gone up 800% since 1993, and that was before cell phone use was as widespread as it is today.

3. Driving requires a person's complete attention.

   Support: Eleanor Phelps was killed in an accident caused when her mother bent over to grab her cell phone and didn't see the light change to red. A truck hit the family van and killed little Eleanor. If her mother had been paying attention, she would have stopped at the light.

Shuffle a Character, page 69

1. My character's job or role: plumber

2. One weird or specific detail about my character: plays the bagpipes

3. Name: Ralph Charles Stevenson

4. Male or female? Male

5. One thing this character wants is: to play the bagpipes full time

6. One thing this character is afraid of is: giving up his day job (plumbing)

7. Write a paragraph describing your character.

   Ralph has been saving all of the money he makes for years, trying to build a nest egg. This way, he hopes he will be able to quit his job as a plumber and find a way to tour the country playing the bagpipes, full-time. After all, he doesn't think there will be a lot of competition for jobs playing the bagpipes.

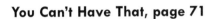

You Can't Have That, page 71

What a character wants, and why	Possible story problems	Conflict (struggle) that might develop
Frank wants a bike so that he doesn't have to walk to school or ride the bus.	He doesn't have the money to buy a bike.	Frank wants to get a job to earn the money, but his parents won't allow it.
Jill wants to go to the movies tonight so she can see Justin, a guy she likes.	She has to stay home and babysit her little sister.	She argues with her parents over her babysitting duties and finally takes her sister to the movies with her, without her parents' permission.
Peter wants to make an A in history class so that he can please his father.	He decides to get a tutor, without telling his father.	Peter's father needs him to help out on the farm after school and is very angry when Peter keeps coming home late.
Liz wants to sneak into an abandoned house to see if it's really haunted.	She sneaks in with a friend, but they don't tell anyone where they are going.	They come face to face with a stray pit bull hiding out in the house.
Mario wants to go out for football because he loves it and is good at it.	He has to take care of his sick grandmother every night after school.	His friends make fun of him for not trying out for the team, thinking that he is afraid to try.

What Are You Afraid Of? page 72

What a character fears, and why	Problem story problems	Conflict (struggle) that might develop
Jill fears the dark because she is afraid of what might lurk there.	She won't go anywhere after dark unless someone is with her.	Her brothers and sisters are tired of having to go with her everywhere and refuse to do it anymore.
Franklin fears eating peanuts because he is allergic to them.	He can't eat at restaurants because most use peanut oil.	A girl he really likes asks him to come to her birthday party at a popular restaurant.
Mr. Miller fears having anyone find out that he can't read because he would be humiliated.	He makes up excuses when his grandchildren ask him to read to them.	His daughter-in-law gets mad at him because she thinks he doesn't want to spend time with his grandchildren.
Merry fears learning to ski because she is so afraid of falling.	Everyone in her family loves to ski, and they all go on frequent trips.	The rest of the family gets mad at her for not even trying.
Jamal fears what his friends will think when they find out he is taking dance lessons.	He has to make up reasons for not hanging out with his friends when he is at his lessons.	His friends think he is snubbing them.

Nice to Meet You, page 74

MAIN CHARACTER

Name	Job or Role	(Optional) Second Job or Role	One Weird Thing or Specific Detail
Sally Willikens	electrician	the avenger	raises chickens

What the Character Wants, and Why	Possible Story Problem	Conflict (Struggle) That Might Develop
For all chicken farms to be humane	A giant corporate chicken farm is moving into the area. All chickens are kept in tiny cages.	Sally tries to get the corporation to change the way it handles the chickens.

OTHER CHARACTERS

Name	Job or Role	(Optional) Second Job or Role	One Weird Thing or Specific Detail
Frank Willikens	Sally's husband	the rational one	He works for the company that does maintenance for the chicken corporation.
Mr. Wheedle	CEO of the corporate chicken farm	the evil one	He has a deep, dark secret.

Thinking Mean, page 76-77

1. Sally, the chicken farmer, wants all chicken farms to use humane practices.

2. A giant corporate chicken farm is moving into the area. All chickens are kept in tiny cages.

3.-4.

   _2_ A. Her husband, Frank, disapproves of Sally's plan to publicize the corporation's inhumane way of caging chickens.

   _3_ B. Sally gets caught trying to free some caged chickens.

   _4_ C. Sally is arrested for barging into Mr. Wheedle's office.

   _1_ D. Mr. Wheedle offers to buy Sally and Frank's farm, in order to expand his farm. His offer is very generous.

5. Yes, the character will successfully overcome the story conflict. Sally will be successful in getting publicity about the corporation's method of caging the chickens. The local community will pressure the corporation into changing its ways by organizing a boycott of chicken from the corporation and getting people in many areas of the country to join the boycott. Sally will also show Mr. Wheedle that he could earn more money for "natural chicken," and she will have research to back up her figures. Finally, the corporation will agree to change its ways and adopt many of Sally's ideas. Mr. Wheedle's deep, dark secret is something Sally will accidentally discover. When she doesn't share the secret with the world, Mr. Wheedle will have new respect for her and will be much more sympathetic to working with her.

Where Am I? page 79

Setting choice: grocery store.

   I wheel my way down an aisle, mesmerized by the brightly colored boxes and jars lined up at attention on the long, endless shelves. I shiver as I bend over the open ice cream bin and try to decide between French vanilla and coffee-caramel-fudge. Then I wheel my way to the mounds of oranges, the piles of carrots and broccoli, and the just-misted lettuce. Where am I?

What's My Mood? page 81

1. Setting: ice cream shop. Mood: happy
3. Yellow and pink balloons floated in the corner at a table filled with giggling children. The delightful smell of the hot fudge sauce wafted from behind the counter, where the servers were dipping their scoops into the cold ice cream. Parents smiled to watch their children's faces light up at the sight of their banana splits. What's my mood?

Writing Your Story, page 83

This will be a story about the character, Sally Willikens, who wants all chicken farms to be humane. However, the character has this main problem: a new corporation is moving into her neighborhood, and this corporation does not treat chickens humanely. And the character is involved in this conflict or struggle: She wants to persuade the chicken corporation to change its ways.

The following complications happen to the main character, from easiest to hardest:

Mr. Wheedle offers to buy Sally and Frank's farm, in order to expand his farm. His offer is very generous.

Her husband, Frank, disapproves of Sally's plan to publicize the corporation's inhumane way of caging chickens.

Sally gets caught trying to free some caged chickens.

Sally is arrested for barging into Mr. Wheedle's office.

Setting: a farm

Mood: tense

Zoom and Pan, page 85

1. An attic

3. Zoom point of view:
   She wiped the dust from the top of the carton, sneezing as the dust tickled her nose. She opened the carton and sorted through the faded newspaper clippings, the ribbons and old wrapping paper, and the old baby shoes and bibs. Finally, at the bottom she found what she had been looking for: her mother's sparkly Miss Atlanta crown.

5. Panorama point of view:
   She opened the door and sighed at the mess.

The attic was filled with junk, floor to ceiling. There were old coats and dresses hanging from clothes racks, rusty old baby strollers, an old crib, shoes tumbling out of boxes, and forgotten toys piled in a corner. There was a musty smell that made her wince as the door creaked shut behind her.

Fools and Noodleheads, page 90

- Ritual opening: Once upon a time
- Fool: Dull Darla
  Smart One: Sharp Shelly
- Problem to be solved: How to toast bread
- Exaggeration:
- Dull Darla hikes to the top of a tall mountain so the bread will be closer to the sun and will toast.

- Dull Darla eats very hot chili peppers and then breathes on her bread to toast it.

- Dull Darla builds a bonfire, puts her bread on a stick, and holds it in the fire.

- Ritual closing: And, as far as anyone knows, they are still toasting their bread in ridiculous ways.

BIBLIOGRAPHY

Pattison, Darcy. *The Journey of Oliver K. Woodman.* Harcourt Children's Books, 2003.

Pattison, Darcy. *The Wayfinder.* New York: Greenwillow, 2000.

Salley, Coleen. *Epossumondas.* Harcourt Children's Books, 2002.

Singer, Isaac Bashevis. *Zlateh the Goat and Other Stories.* Harper Collins, 2001.

QUICK REFERENCE

Many of the activities in *Paper Lightning* will become basic tools in your students' writing toolkit and are, therefore, likely to be used frequently. For ease of reference, here are the page numbers of these student activities:

Basic
- Sensory Word Bank, pages 27-28
- Packed With Facts Word Bank, pages 33-34

Non-fiction
- What Is My Opinion?, pages 58-59
- Making Reasons Believable, pages 61-62

Fiction
- You Can't Have That!, page 71
- What Are You Afraid Of?, page 72
- Nice to Meet You, page 74
- Thinking Mean, pages 76-77
- Writing Your Story, page 83

ABOUT THE AUTHOR

Darcy Pattison is the author of *The Journey of Oliver K. Woodman* (Harcourt), *Searching for Oliver K. Woodman* (Harcourt) and *19 Girls and Me* (Philomel/Penguin). For over 20 years, she has taught writing and professional teacher development classes. She lives in Arkansas.